Terrorist Attack Girl

(Meyli Chapin)

Cover design by KD.

First edition November 2021.

ISBN-13: 9798497395075 (paperback)
ISBN-13: 9798499278048 (hardcover)

To my heroes:

Obi Wan Nairobi and the other brave men who physically pulled me out of the hotel that day, and my family, friends and therapists, who have mentally pulled me out of that hotel every day since.

I have changed the names and identities of many of the people herein to protect their privacy.

Table of Contents

Letter to the Reader

I never meant to write a book.

I wrote because I didn't know what else to do. I wrote when I was terrified, when I couldn't sleep, when I didn't understand what was happening to me, when I couldn't stop the flashbacks. I wrote all the time, to try to get all the bad things out of my head and onto the paper. It didn't get them out of my head, really, but it did help a little.

There were two documents on my laptop at first. In one, I wrote about the terrorist attack in great detail. Every single piece of it, everything I could remember. The smells, the sounds, the fear, the texts I sent, everything. I wanted to physically separate it from myself. Extricate it from my being. Exorcise it perhaps.

The other document was my running journal. I would write how I was feeling in the aftermath, often just ranting about how confused or broken I felt. It is a log of exactly what was happening in my brain, detailed to the best of my ability. It is a very raw and honest look into my mind, in all its shattered glory, after I lived.

Several months after the attack, when therapy was finally starting to make a real difference in my life, I realized they were the same story: that of my survival. I was almost murdered in the attack, and then after, I wanted to take my own life because I no longer recognized myself, my life, or my mind. I went from needing to figure out how to physically survive, to needing to learn how to mentally survive.

That mental fallout is a reality of terrorism, and of trauma at large. But it's a reality we rarely talk about. For me, that's why this book became important. It's not because I think my story is particularly interesting, and unfortunately, it's not even all that uncommon. People are traumatized by horrible events all over the world every single day. The only difference is that I happen to have this in-depth record of what both elements of survival were really like. So, I combined the two documents into this book so that readers can understand what both battles for survival were like. The journal entries are in here, verbatim, in italics, side by side with the record of the trauma itself.

I think too often the stories of survivors are shortened on their behalf; we hear that someone survived something terrible and now they are a motivational speaker or race car driver or extraordinary athlete. Those stories are beautiful and inspirational, but they are also censored in a way. What happened between those two points? What happened after the terrible thing but before the person stepped into the spotlight as an inspiration? I'd be willing to bet it was an incredible, Herculean struggle. A battle of wills inside oneself, fighting against the resounding shockwaves of the trauma and the mind it left in ruins to make oneself whole again. To make light in the darkness. To even believe that there could be light again. And by leaving out that part of the story, I think we do a disservice to anyone who is struggling, or ever has. And unfortunately, that is almost all of us. To quote a very sad statistic, the majority of Americans will have survived at least one acute trauma by the time they are 45 years old.

Mine happened when I was 26. I am lucky it's only been the one so far. But I want to open my mind and my heart to you and look back at that time because I want to tell my own story in my own words, the way it really happened. Darkness, ugliness and all. Because it's the truth. The whole truth.

So, if you ever hear someone else tell my story the short way, saying that I went on to start a company and help people after I lived through a terrorist attack, just remember what happened in between. And if you're currently struggling, know that it's ok, and there really is a light at the end of the tunnel. Even if you feel beaten, and you're crawling over the sharp gravel at the bottom of the tunnel, dragging yourself along and stopping every few feet to cry, scraping your knees, bloody and dirty, know that it's natural. Bad things happen to us, and they can be really hard to deal with, not just physically but also mentally. Let yourself struggle and let yourself cry. And then keep crawling and getting stronger and looking for that light.

Never lose hope.

Prologue

Twelve weeks after the terrorist attack, my therapist asked me where I see myself at the end of this. The end of my journey to heal, the end of Prolonged Exposure treatment. I shook my head and told her there is only one thing I really want: I want to be *better*. I want to stop being "Terrorist Attack Girl" and just be Meyli again. I want to remember what it's like not to have every single new experience be colored by this one event in my life; I want to have a conversation with someone where I can tell they aren't holding back or altering what they say out of pity or concern. I want to have a handle on my emotions again, a handle on my identity. I want to remember how it feels to be myself, and forget this whole horrible thing ever happened.

My therapist told me she imagined it differently. She said she could see me at the end of this with a cape, a cape sporting the name Terrorist Attack Girl. And she could see me having the strength to take what happened in the hotel that day and turn it into hope and help for others. That instead of wishing this had never happened to me, I would find a way to harness it as my own little superpower.

Today I say to that therapist: Thank you for always helping me see the light in the darkest hours. You saved me and you gave me hope.

To everyone else I say: Hi. You can call me Terrorist Attack Girl.

Part One:
Suicide Bomber

Y ou can do a lot in seventeen hours. A lot. On a typical day, I might wake up at 8am, pick out my clothes, get ready, kiss my fiancé, Paul, goodbye (which will inevitably prompt me to consider calling in sick), then eventually let reality set in that I am going to be late if I wait much longer to leave, get in my car and drive to work. And that's just one hour. I would have a full work day, take tons of meetings, respond to dozens of emails, check on wedding plans over lunch, work out, shower, order groceries, head home, cook dinner, eat dinner while watching a show with Paul, finish the show, then we would tell each other all about our days, and that would still only be twelve hours. Maybe after that we would kiss a little and snuggle in front of the fireplace. Thirteen hours. Which means I would still have four hours left. I could watch two movies or work on my novel or chat with a friend for a bit, or all of the above. Four hours is a long time. But seventeen hours, seventeen hours is a really long time. Even as I tell you all of this, I know you can't really understand how long it can be. Because until I spent seventeen hours on the bathroom floor of my hotel room while terrorists tried to kill me, I never understood how long sev-

enteen hours was either.

I wasn't supposed to be there. I was supposed to be at an interview with my research team, asking local citizens questions about how they use their phones. In my role at Google, this was a pretty standard project, with a fairly normal international itinerary. I had spent the previous week in Mumbai doing the same before arriving in Nairobi, Kenya. I spent my first day there in a village made mostly of corrugated sheets of metal, giving interviews and playing tag with small children who didn't speak a word of English, had never seen the type of technology we carried with us for the recordings we were making. I had texted my parents, telling them the infrastructure was wonderful, that my private driver was remarkably kind, and that the DusitD2, the five-star hotel Google had instructed me to book, was lovely indeed. I knew that they had been worrying about me as I traveled, and I joked with them that there had certainly been no need to do so. On the second morning, my driver had taken me to the must-see tourist sites: the baby elephant sanctuary, and the park where you can handfeed giraffes before enjoying a scenic lunch. Afterward, we were supposed to head to more interviews, but the traffic had backed up; it was too congested in the city center. We would be an hour late to an hour and a half interview. I decided it wasn't worth it; the hotel was much closer, and he could just drop me there for a nap until I met back up with my team later that evening. The jet lag you experience on the far side of the planet is truly extraordinary - it was only 3pm but I had already been awake for twelve hours. I started texting my dad – it was funny that he was even awake, the time difference was considerable, and it was still quite early in Ohio. He told me that he couldn't sleep; a family dispute had been bothering him acutely and he was feeling quite anxious about it. At the same time, I had been packing my things. I had a flight scheduled the next morning to South Africa where I would meet Paul. He is a private pilot and we planned to take a few days of vacation, meet there, and fly around in bush planes trying to spot the Big Five. I was incredibly excited and wanted all of my things packed up and ready to go so that after my nap I could grab dinner, sleep a few hours and then head to the airport without any delays. While I was reorganizing my little carry-ons (I always travel lightly, especially when it's international), I found the small, felt gift bag I had received from my hotel in India upon checking out. Idly, I opened it in between sending texts to my dad, and I found a little wooden beaded bracelet with a note that said something about the keepsake bringing me luck and prosperity. It reminded me of my dad as he usually wears a very similar bracelet, so I put it on, sent him a picture and said, "Look, we match!" Then, bags neatly packed, I took off my bra, but left on my day clothes as I still had that dinner to attend and hopped in bed. So that's what I was doing when the first bomb went off, lying down for a nap.

I relive that conversation with my driver all the time. It was about two hours before the attack, and he was taking me for lunch. He was incredibly kind. He wasn't just showing me around, he was also teaching me about Kenya's history, particularly the last couple of decades' worth. He even told me about his own family, about how he supported the children of a dead sibling as well as his own. About how that wasn't

3

unusual in that part of the world. About how he just wanted to keep them fed with a roof over their heads. He told me about the immense corruption in his country, how it runs as deep as it does wide. How you can complain or lobby against the politicians, but you'll simply end up in jail because the police are in their pockets. He drove me by massive compounds with astounding mansions on them, surrounded by huge, impenetrable fences and told me that was where the politicians lived. I was astounded – in a country with so much poverty, how could the politicians stand to live like that? Weren't they ashamed? He drove me by Nairobi's sprawling, seemingly endless slum. That was how the people lived, as the politicians enjoyed their mansions. It was sickening. But the worst thing he told me was about Kenya's dispute with Somalia. How Kenyan forces are in Somalia trying to tamp down resistance, trying to impede the Islamic extremist group there in their efforts to form a caliphate. But this infuriates the Somalian extremists, so they retaliate with terror attacks. I was shocked at my own ignorance. I was not in Syria or Afghanistan. I did not know terrorist attacks happened in the likes of Kenya. He told me how these Somalian rebels had, in the preceding few years, attacked a mall just across town, and a college campus as well. Stunned, I asked him if he thought there was still a real threat of terrorism in his country. He responded, "Absolutely." I was amazed by how calmly he said that. Didn't he want to move? How terrifying to live under that threat every day. I asked him if he wished the Kenyan forces would pull out of Somalia to end this terror, and he said no, because that would be far worse. I was impressed by his courage. Also, in the back of my head, I was thankful to be getting the hell out of that country the next morning. Terrorist attacks? Jesus

Christ.

My head had barely hit the pillow when the building exploded. It's hard to tell you what it was like in a way that can convey it properly. It was genuinely like nothing I had ever heard before in my life. The sound was so loud that I realize now I was deaf for some moments afterward which is why I didn't hear any screams. Even my own. I immediately started screaming, "No!" I repeated this over and over because what you may not understand is that when part of your hotel explodes, there is no question. There is no part of your brain that tries to suggest that perhaps someone just dropped something downstairs, or perhaps a car backfired. That first explosion shook my floor, my bed, my body. It rattled my bones and it deafened me. It was clear in that instant that a bomb had gone off, quite literally, just outside my room.

My life now is in two parts: Before Terrorist Attack (BTA) and After Terrorist Attack (ATA). Tragedy like that, trauma like that, strikes an impenetrable line in the cement, a tattoo that never fades, separating who you were then from who you are now. An event like that crushes your sense of self, your beliefs about the world, and sometimes, your will to live. It holds you to a higher standard than you ever thought possible, demanding of you every day: what will you do now? What will you make of the tatters of your life? Is it even worth putting back together?

I knew which direction the explosion had come from, as I instinctively ran for the window, still screaming, that faced the courtyard. I fumbled with the curtains for a few seconds that felt like an eternity, before tearing them open. But I couldn't understand the scene outside. Smoke was rolling through the courtyard in a way that looked absurdly like a movie. There was a tint on the glass which made everything look like it was being seen through a sepia tone lens. And my shaking hands and screaming mouth and absolute terror made everything feel like it was in slow motion for those twenty seconds or so while I tried to understand what I was seeing. There were chunks of a human body, surrounded by blood spray scattered throughout the courtyard. There was a leg, a recognizable human leg, that had been part of a living human person just moments before. Tatters of clothing were still stuck to it, and it was surrounded by blood and torn flesh. But when you have never seen something like that before in real life, you can't understand it in that first instant. It has no place in your mind or your consciousness. It does not belong in the world of true and tangible things; it can only happen on your TV, or in a world of fiction. People don't really walk into your hotel and blow themselves up. Except that they do. So, no matter how many times I closed my eyes and shook my head and then opened them again, those chunks of human flesh, scraps of cloth still adhered to them, were there, in the courtyard, in front of my eyes, in sepia tone.

It's physically sickening to write this. It's so hard. To try to tell you what I have learned in the aftermath, I also have to try to convey the worst seventeen hours of my life. And to write it like this is to relive it. To review my notes and texts, my memories and phone calls, is to throw myself right back into that hotel. It's to shake on the bathroom floor and scream and cry and beg someone, anyone, to come help. It's to curse myself for going on that trip to Africa in the first place. It's to accept my death and just hope that it is quick. It is to torture my parents and family through seventeen hours of uncertainty while they wonder if I will die, and if so, how? Will it be violent? Will it be slow? Will they end up watching it on the news? It's to think about how they're thinking about how scared and alone I am. And how I will die that way, most likely: scared and alone. And it's to remember that feeling, as I thought that if I did die there, it would ruin their lives. They would never be the same. And it would all be my fault.

Just as my brain started to process how very real that scene outside my window was, I looked left, and saw two large men dressed in dark, matching outfits coming around the corner and into the courtyard with AK47s. I knew immediately, instinctively even, that they were not police. Perhaps it was because they were not shouldering their guns but firing into the decimation, that I knew they were terrorists. Perhaps it was because they passed through the blood spatter of their former friend without so much as looking around. Perhaps it was because they were walking, not running, and moving toward the explosion not away. Perhaps it was the look of apathy and determination on their faces, which betrayed the fact that the bomb had not taken them by surprise, as it had the rest of us. I knew instantly: these men, who were complete strangers to me, were here to kill me. To kill all of us.

How do you explain it to people? How do you face your

7

colleagues or acquaintances and tell them, 'Oh yes, well I am mostly okay. Except for the flashbacks. And the nightmares. And my fear of what humanity can be. And my panic attacks. And my random fits of sobbing. And my inability to focus or process or read. Or go to work. Or be myself. Or go to the airport. Or the gym. Or the grocery store.' How do you tell the people who used to know you that even though you have only been out of the US for two weeks, and you look exactly the same, you aren't who you were anymore? How do you take the shattered pieces of your life and figure out what in the fuck to do with them? How do you crawl out of bed on the days that you just want to crawl into a hole? How do you face the fact that it wasn't even close to over after seventeen long hours? That even though you're physically ok, your mind is so totally fucked up that you don't even feel like a shadow of your former self, which is so incredibly frustrating that it makes you feel like you are going mad? How do you act like you believe them when they tell you that you will be ok?

The panic is also hard to explain but suffice it to say my entire body was shaking uncontrollably. I could barely close my curtains and sprint over to my two cell phones (one work, one personal). I could barely send off the goodbye texts to my parents and Paul saying that terrorists were attacking my hotel, and that I loved them. I remember these scenes only in small clips, as if there are entire minutes of utter blackness between them, though I know of course that that's not true. It is odd to try to remember, precisely, scene-to-scene, how you said goodbye to your loved ones in what you genuinely believed were your last moments. It's hard to explain how the word 'terror' is overused, because until that moment I'd had absolutely no basis for feeling anything remotely close to it. It's uncomfortable to describe to you how completely *not* brave I was. How much like a hunted animal I was. Backed into a corner, wanting only to leave with my life, and sure that I never would. It's absolutely debilitating to relive it.

These days are hard for me, but with a lining of beauty that gives me joy in a way I had never felt before. That is the flip side of terror, the flip side of having had your life threatened for seventeen straight hours while you cowered in a bathroom. The feeling of immense joy over tiny moments in life that you never would have thought to appreciate before. It's the tears of joy I cried four days ATA as Paul and I ran through the Ohio snow at eleven o'clock at night, the wind lapping at our cheeks like ice cold waves, our footprints making beautiful, unique, temporary art in the fresh powder that had never been made to look exactly like that before, and never will again. It is two weeks ATA when, after a bout of immense depression where I could not get off my floor for two days, too terrified of the entire world and too frustrated with humanity to do anything but cry, I went to the gym in a fit of rage, and then afterward finally felt some much-needed relief. In that moment, I asked Paul to dance with me in the kitchen, and he did. I did not feel joy, but elation, at being alive, there in that moment, and being able to touch this amazing man, this rock in my life, who I came so close to not getting to marry. And in each moment of immense joy, I take back a little piece of what the terrorists stole from me that day.

When the gunshots started, I couldn't move. I never

9

would have thought four guns could make that much noise; the sounds were reverberating off of every wall, slamming themselves around inside my brain, screaming, "DANGER!" I was picturing tons of them, the terrorists I had just seen, surrounding us on all sides, flowing into the hotel, so many of them. There was no one to stop them. Their plan was too good. They had us trapped, like animals, and they would come through and systematically execute us, room by room. It was the first moment where I was no longer confused, I was completely certain of what was happening. The terror took over, it gripped me from the inside. My heart was beating so hard it was legitimately painful, and I felt like the terror might strike me dead on the spot, might cause my heart to explode before the terrorists even made it to my room. My mouth was completely dry, and my lungs felt like a hand had reached inside my chest and placed a vice grip on them. I couldn't breathe, I couldn't think, I couldn't move. The terror had taken over completely. There was nothing strong or brave in it, I was stripped of everything, and all that was left was pure terror and adrenaline and the desire to flee. But there was nothing to do. There was nowhere to go. I couldn't run, or scream, or hide. They would find me. They would find us all. I recognized, even though I wanted more than anything to reject it, that my life was over. They would win. They already had.

ATA, here is what I want: I want my life back, I want my love of travel back, my naïveté, my sense of trust, my ability to sleep peacefully. I want to unsee what I've seen. I want a new job where I can actually change the world, but it's hard to imagine because I am so overwhelmed with how fucked the world is. I want not to feel or see that anymore. Or I want the world to just not be so fucked up anymore. I want to see things the way I used to: clear, black and white, nothing too difficult to overcome. I want to believe that humans are mostly good, the way I used to. I want to feel the way I used to feel each day when I woke up, with joy and a smile, taking in the sunshine and thinking that the world was my oyster. I want my biggest realistic fear to be that I won't do well in my next performance review at work, though even that was never that realistic, I guess. I want to feel invincible again, unstoppable. I used to believe a little grit and fortitude could get me through anything. Now I don't even know if I want to get through.

But that was the most horrific part of all: it wasn't over instantly. I knew they had begun the executions; I could hear them downstairs murdering people in cold blood, but there was nothing I could do, and they weren't at my room yet. So, I had to wait. Just stand there, and know they were coming for me, listen to them on their way, and just wait for them to show up. That's all that was left of my life, these moments of pure terror. Did I have seconds left? Minutes? I knew it was somewhere in that range. And it dawned on me that I had to say goodbye to my family. It was time. Because when it processed that this was the very end of my life, that I would die alone and afraid, halfway around the world, that strangers would riddle my body with bullets and leave me there to bleed out, it also dawned on me that my family, every single person I had ever loved, was being ripped away from me. And I had mere moments to send my final words to them. What do you say?

Directly after the attack, I really wanted my engagement ring. Desperately. As if, somehow, that was proof that I was no longer traveling somewhere dangerous, because I could again wear a diamond ring, which would thereby make me safe. Or convince me I was safe. Or something. But when I finally got it, it just felt hollow. It was not Paul, the man who held me each night as I woke in a cold sweat from nightmares. It was just an empty symbol which we had imbued, incorrectly, with meaning.

I opened my text conversation with my dad. I saw the picture of the bracelet. I froze for a single instant, completely confused as to how I was so safe just ten minutes before that I had sent something so lighthearted, and now I had to say goodbye. But there was no time to wonder how this had happened. How my life had been ripped away from me in a mere moment. I would miss my chance to say goodbye. I just told him there was a terrorist attack on the hotel, and that I love him. Because I knew that if there was one last thing, I wanted my family to hear from me, it was 'I love you.' I really, really did. I thought perhaps it would comfort them, knowing that was my last thought before I died. It didn't comfort me. It was all the more horrific that I loved them so much, loved my life so much, and it was going to be extinguished in a fucking hotel room in Africa. It was a goddamn shame. No one should have to die like that. I repeated the text and sent it to Paul, but the words felt empty, hollow. He was so much to me, he was the man I was going to marry, the man I so wanted to marry. He was my shield and haven. He always kept me safe and happy. And to say goodbye like that, with the same words I say to relatives, it was wrong, too shallow. So, I quickly added, 'More than anything.' And I wished desperately that when he saw it, he would understand all the meaning I had intended to convey. All the eloquent, beautiful things that I didn't have time to say. How much I was wishing, when I sent it, that I was safe and sound with him, in his arms, where nothing bad could reach me. But time was ticking, my death was nearing, so I sent the next text to my mom. And then I hesitated for an instant; I wasn't sure if I should text my baby brother. He was in his first year of college. He was happy-go-lucky and discovering himself and loving all of his classes and making new friends. I didn't want him anywhere near the horror I was facing. I didn't text him. He knew I loved him. Let him hear about all of this when it was over. When they were shipping my bullet-ridden body back to the US for burial. Let him not know until it was all over. So that was it. I had said goodbye. And I thought that maybe after that I would feel brave. I would face my death calmly, like they do in the movies. Accept it and widen my arms to bring on the bullets. But it wasn't like that. There wasn't a bit of bravery in it. I stood there, shaking, waiting for them to knock down my door. My mind raced desperately, wondering if there was anything I could say to them to keep them from killing me. What if I begged, bartered, greeted them with a customary Muslim greeting? Was there anything I could do? I so badly wanted to live. And so completely knew that I wouldn't.

I think often about how glad I am that Paul was not there with me. People find that surprising. They think that I would have done anything to have some comfort, have someone to hold me or tell me it was going to be ok. But just the thought

13

of him being in that situation makes my heart race and my stomach turn. I would not wish a terrorist attack on my worst enemy. It's nothing that a human being should ever have to go through. How, then, could I ever wish it on the person I love most? I am so thankful that he did not see me fall apart. That he did not experience the terror I did. That he did not have to feel responsible for our lives. That we did not have to see each other cowering on the bathroom floor. But I also want to make something clear. The fact that Paul was not there does not mean he cannot handle the details. From the bathroom, I texted him, "There's an exploded body in the courtyard." He did not balk but tried to comfort me. In the aftermath, I have told him far more. I have told him the most sordid details; I have told him about my most intimate moments in therapy, I have told him everything. Because if I hid things from him in an effort to protect him, I would put a wall up between us. It would irrevocably harm our relationship. I have to trust that he can handle it, that he wants to help me shoulder this burden. I lost enough in the attack that day, I won't let it harm what we have.

Let me tell you some of the things I didn't think about during the attack. Certain misnomers you believe you will think about in a near-death situation, these romanticized moments where, you've been told, life flashes before your eyes or you recall your fondest childhood memories. It doesn't happen that way. I never thought it might be a nightmare, I just wished it was. I never thought about my past in any form, except for replaying that day over and over and thinking about all the things I could have done differently to not have ended up in the hotel at the time the terrorists arrived. To berate myself and cry because I hadn't gone exploring or out to meet my team. To insult my own idiocy for putting myself there, for abdicating my own fucking life. But I didn't remember anything from my childhood. I didn't look at the background on my phone (a photo of me with my brother and Paul) and cry longingly for my loved ones. No part of my life 'flashed before my eyes' in any way, shape or form. There was no excess capacity in my brain for luxuries like that. When people describe fight or flight mode, they should explain that it completely overtakes all other functionality. I had very little ability to be rational, and without realizing it I would go a long time without responding to texts from my loved ones, because I was too busy hunched on the floor trying to plan an escape route, or find an incredible hiding place that would never reveal that a human had ever set foot in that hotel room. I was pure adrenaline and absolute fear. I felt no hunger, no thirst, and despite having been awake for well over twelve hours even when it started, I felt no desire to sleep. I felt only the desire to figure out a way to escape with my life.

Every week ATA: Were you scared? Did you see them? What did you hear? Were you cold? Are you ok? Do you still think about it? Are you working? Why does PTSD mean you can't work? But what do you do all day now? So, you were in your hotel room the whole time? Do you have nightmares? Are you going to go back to your job? Were you by yourself? Did you hide? Did you see anyone die? Did you know anyone else in the hotel? Did you think you were going to die?

Well. Given that I am your personal circus freak, let me come up with some answers for you.

I knew what would happen next, and I saw it a million times. I knew that any second, they would knock my door down, maybe with boots, or fists, or maybe with explosives. They would be screaming in a language I couldn't understand and waving their huge guns in my face. I would sink to my knees, sobbing, pleading for my life. And they wouldn't care. Maybe they would even enjoy killing me more, because I was so scared, because I wasn't brave. They would scream and the bullets would start. The gunshots would be deafening, and I would feel the metal fragments ripping through my body, all over. There would be so many of the men, shooting me all at once. But somehow, body full of lead, I wouldn't die instantly. I would tip over backwards, slowly, blood gurgling in the back of my throat as my life seeped out of me and onto the hotel room floor. My limbs would end up all splayed out, soaked with blood, and the terrorists would look satisfied. They would hustle out of my room, and on to the next one. They had to kill everyone, not just me. And that would be the very last thing I would see, the men who had taken my life moving on to the next room to take more. What a horrible final sight. And I would die there, right where they left me. I saw it so many times just in those first few moments that by the end of seventeen hours it would feel like it had been burned into my brain. It would take months to undo the hundreds of deaths I had died there, in my head. It would take months to come all the way back to life. And it would take months to realize there were little parts of me that *had* died there, in all that terror, in all those imagined deaths, that I would never, ever be able to get back.

8 weeks ATA: Paul cried when he told me what the attack was like for him, which surprised me because during the experience he was so calm. But that's the whole point. He didn't really get to experience his feelings while it was happening, so it is in retrospect that he feels the pain and fear he couldn't let himself feel at the time. He told me that after the initial shock, and rereading my first text a few times, his brain shut off his emotional response for the remainder of the attack and went into solution mode. He started to mentally iterate on anything he could do to help me, to save my life. He considered borrowing a South African airplane and flying to Nairobi himself, but quickly realized he wouldn't be able to do any actual good that way, and it would require him to be out of touch for an extended period of time which was unacceptable. So, he moved into the realm where he felt he could contribute immediately and with impact: providing information. For the majority of the attack, Paul was my conduit to important information. He contacted every single person in our immediate and even distant network with any sort of governmental connection or import. He talked to friends in the military or with security clearances, folks at the Embassy, and most importantly my uncle in the Secret Service who helped us immensely. We still talk about all of those folks, and how thankful we are for any and all information they provided, even when that was just that I should continue to shelter in my room and not try to flee. Paul gathered this info and passed it to me calmly and collectedly for all seventeen hours. He relayed similar information to my parents and talked them down from panic multiple times. He was like an information command center for all of us the whole time and having such a central role kept his emotions at bay and gave him a more important focus. Every once in a while, when I'd go too long without texting him, the panic would start to creep in, but he never let himself break. He never texted me anything like, "Are you still alive?!" Though he often wanted to. He was an absolute rock the entire time. He told me he never cried while I was in the attack, never even considered it. I don't know what any of us would have done without him. But these days are harder. These days he is overly protective, and he panics when either of us has to travel, or if I go too long without texting him. He is calmest when I am immediately next to him, when he can reach out and touch me, assuring himself that I am not in danger, that I am not dead. When he does not have to be the information command center, from a different country, hoping desperately that some piece of information he can get his hands on will keep me from being violently murdered in a hotel bathroom in Kenya.

The gunshots were infinite. The explosions never stopped. I don't mean to say that neither of those ever let up at all, I just mean to say that for seventeen hours I heard gunshots and heard and felt explosions. Sometimes there were lulls, but they were never over. Never. At one point, as the sun was coming up, the birds came back. They sat in the trees right outside my room and, as if nothing had ever happened, they began their songs. I shook my head because it felt impossible to hear birds chirping as the sun came up, but still know that my life was hanging in the balance. But the birds weren't there for long before the explosions started again and they scattered, squawking at the impertinence of humans.

5 weeks ATA: I found deep solace today. I talked to our

friends who are in the military. They had no morbid curiosity prompting them to ask about the worst details of my experience; they have seen war up close for themselves. They were not awed; they did not treat me like a freak show in a circus. They did not mince their words, and they did not look at me with pity. They heard me out, and they empathized and shared similar stories of war and what it does to people. They asked about my PTSD symptoms like it was the most normal thing in the world. They shared some of the issues they'd had after their first tours in the Middle East and it was like I was in an alternate universe where everything I am experiencing makes sense. They talked about how they couldn't bond with their loved ones when they first got back, how they blatantly disrespected authority and nonsensical rules, how they resented how easy things are here and people whose most difficult decision today will be which brand of chips to buy. They explained that suddenly they had had a hard time relating to the culture that had always been theirs. In fact, they had reverse culture shock. And while everyone else was laughing and enjoying their freedom, these two had been thinking about the cost of that freedom. And that had kept them from being able to fit in the way they had before. It was like they could see into my mind and my heart and my soul. And for the first time since getting back, I felt like maybe I could still fit in somewhere. Like there is a tiny little paradise where I can hide away sometimes and forget what it's like to be a freak.

I have to tell you about the room where I would spend the next seventeen hours of my life, the worst seventeen hours of my life. It is tough to think back on it, draw it out like this for you, in distant and removed words, so that you can picture it. I don't want you to picture it, don't want to picture it myself. It stands out in my mind as a foul place, even though on the surface it is as innocuous as any other hotel room. But for you to understand the story, for you to sit there with me for seventeen hours, I guess you have to understand where you are sitting. The room itself was not remarkable in any way, especially for a five-star hotel. The design decisions were simple, modern. There were clean horizontal and vertical lines everywhere, the colors almost completely restricted to neutrals: blacks, beiges and browns on everything, with hints of orange in tiny corners barely visible in the dim lighting. The carpet in the bedroom was simple, elegant: a neutral beige with a pattern of clean, parallel dark lines. The bed was oddly low, white linens standing out starkly in the dark room. It was surrounded by a few pragmatic pieces of furniture, a nightstand, reading chair, and book table, modern vertical lamps installed into the wall. It was clear that someone had tried hard to make sure the room did not feel cluttered. There was a built-in desk made of dark wood and topped with a beige counter and black pad for comfortable working, a gray rolling chair waiting beneath it, a flat screen TV hovering above. Attached to the desk was a small coffee station, made of the same dark wood and beige counter material, topped with the coffee and tea accoutrement. Underneath was a minibar that was sealed into a desk-like façade, presumably so that it didn't look cheap or tacky.

The only truly bright thing in the room was next to the coffee station - it was a rainbow-colored elephant in a transparent box. I had picked it up the day before, opened the box, read its little description. It was made of recycled flip flops, and if you wanted, you could take it home and it would automatically be charged to your bill. I had thought about it - I really thought it was neat and I loved the bright colors, but I couldn't have fit it in my carry-on bags if I had tried. To the right of the elephant was a little hallway. The carpet gave way to massive beige tiles there, the color scheme fitting seamlessly with the rest of the room. There was a door there too, to a small balcony you could step out on where you could look out over the courtyard. I had done that the day before as well, the slight pollution in the air singeing my nose before I decided to go back into the room and seal the door up. My suitcase was on a little luggage rack in a nook just by that door, and across from it was a long row of dark wooden slatted doors, which slid to reveal a closet, laundry bag and safe waiting patiently inside. I had locked my valuables in the safe the day before and had filled the laundry bag and sent it off just that morning. I wouldn't see those clothing items again for weeks.

Then there was the bathroom. Oh god, the bathroom. The bathroom was simple like the rest of the room, the same color scheme and modern design aesthetic very much present. The big beige tile continued from the hallway, except for on the floor of the shower, where there was a pattern of smaller tiles, in different hues of beige and brown. The shower was on the left when you walked in, surrounded only by a transparent glass border to keep the water from leaking into the rest of the bathroom. Interestingly, to get to the bathtub, you had to walk through the shower, past the glass, to where the tub was situated right against the wall, under a massive frosted glass window. (Did you know that in emergencies, they tell you stay away from the windows and hide in the bathtub? The set-up of this bathroom, however, rendered that impossible.) To the right of the shower was the vanity, which had dark wooden shelves beneath it where clean towels and a hair dryer waited to be used, a built-in magnifying circular mirror on the wall, and the rectangular white porcelain sink adorning the top neatly, mimicking the shape of the counter it was set upon. A massive mirror backed the vanity, and a vertical light hung on the wall on each side, reminiscent of the ones encasing the bed. A small round trash can was tucked just under the bottom shelf, and I had placed my travel neck pillow next to it (it wouldn't fit inside) as I had dropped it the day before and it seemed gross as well as inefficient to keep traveling with it now that it was dirty. If you continued panning right from the vanity and trash can, you'd see a small beige half-wall, sadly attempting (and failing) to obscure the toilet from view. The toilet was a classic white porcelain one, with the fancy silver flush buttons on the wall, one smaller, one larger. And then there was the phone mounted to the wall next to the toilet, black, classic, a thing I always forget about in hotels, barely see, but which is always present just there, next to the toilet, in case of emergencies. How ironic, how important that phone would become to me, in the case of my emergency. The phone was mounted directly onto the wall that shared a side with the hallway, from which you would enter the room. And that was it. That was my entire set for the worst day of my life. Every single thing that was available to me, every possible hiding place, every resource I might use for salvation. If only I had known.

8 weeks ATA: No one tells you about the nightmares. PTSD means nightmares. In addition to the flashbacks when you're awake. The terror at unexpected loud noises. The inability to go out in public. The fear that the terrorists will find you even in your home country. The panic attacks. The inability to focus or do work. The rage you take out on your family and friends. But for me, the worst is the nightmares. I have 1-2 nightmares per night. Each is tied to my experience in that hotel but is not a reliving of exactly what happened. There is always a twist. In one, I am in a hotel room, but it's different than the one I was actually in, and some of my friends are there. When the explosion goes off, I know exactly what's happening and I snap into solution mode. I somehow find a way to take apart the couch and hide inside of it moments before the terrorists break the door down. I am shaking and scared, but I know I have a great hiding place. It is only then, though, that I remember my friends. My friends! Where are they hiding? Is it good enough? Will the terrorists find them? But my friends aren't used to terrorist attacks, they didn't know how to hide well enough. I watch from the couch as the terrorists drag my friends out the door, but I am frozen in place. I cannot move or speak. I wake in a cold sweat, and don't even bother trying to go back to sleep. Who would want to sleep if that's what they see when their eyes are closed? The next night, the twist is that I am in a gymnasium with tons of other people, many of whom are children. The terrorists are striding around the gym and pointing to people at random. They make them stand up, only to be executed, firing-squad style. They walk up to me, but they point to a small group of children directly next to me. I watch as they put holes through these children's heads. This night I wake up screaming. That's it for sleep once again. The next night the twist is that we are in the streets of Nairobi, and my mother is there. The terrorists explain to us calmly that they are going to kill me. But when they raise their AKs to shoot, my mother jumps in front of me at the last moment to take the bullets herself. I watch her blood spill all over the dirt. I wake in terror once again. The nightmares make me afraid to go to sleep. If I am lucky, I sleep a few hours before one strikes. On average I get two to four hours of sleep per night. I was never a great sleeper, I used to sleep around seven hours per night, usually taking a sleep aide a few times a year to help when I was really stressed about work. But that has nothing on how this feels. I have no escape; in the toughest battle of my life, I am unable to ever recharge. I constantly feel like I am running on fumes, and then somehow the tank gets even emptier, though I was already sure there was nothing left. I am exhausted and extremely short-tempered during the days. I am aware that I lack a basic capability for reason and objective thought. My moods swing like crazy and I have dark circles under my eyes. The lack of sleep is really taking its toll, and I don't know how much more I can take. But it's also fucked up, because despite how much I need sleep, I don't want to sleep. I know the nightmares will come and it's hard to feel like the sleep would be worth it, much less restful. I try to add a one- or two-hour nap during the day, when it's light out. It's funny, terrorists don't wait until it's dark to attack, I know that, but somehow, when it's light out, I don't have the nightmares as much.

I guess you want to know what happened next. After the man blew himself up in the courtyard restaurant, and the others followed in his blood-spatter to gun us down.

After I texted the people I love to tell them just that before I could be killed. Next, I called Google's emergency security line - it was the only emergency number I knew I could call from another country - and tried to explain what was going on. I don't remember what I said, only that my voice shook uncontrollably. I don't even remember deciding to call, only that my hands were shaking so badly I could barely get the number dialed. I do remember that the woman who answered had to transfer me to someone else, and that for some reason in that moment, that seemed absolutely bizarre. Why wouldn't the person who answers the phone be equipped to deal with my situation when time was so clearly of the essence? When I had so few precious moments left in my life?

2 weeks ATA: My life used to be normal, unremarkable. I miss that. I was born and raised in a small town in Ohio; my dad is from that same small town and my mom is from Puerto Rico. My household was multicultural, our walls were painted bright orange and yellow and green, the smell of churrasco always wafted over from the kitchen, and my mom's telenovelas blared from the next room. We were not well off when I was young, in fact we were on welfare when I was a small child, but no matter what was going on financially, one thing was always true: the priority for the family was my education. My mom used to go into my public schools and chastise my teachers for not challenging me enough, make them give me extra assignments and more advanced reading material. My dad filled our shelves with every kind of book you can imagine and would read to me from the classics until I fell asleep each night, dreaming of Huck Finn, Scout, Tom Sawyer and all the others. By the

*time I was eighteen, my parents had started their own busi-
nesses, the quintessential story of the American Dream becoming their reality, and had saved enough to send me to
Stanford. The rules were that if I did not keep a 3.9+ GPA
they would not pay for my tuition, and that anything beyond
tuition was my responsibility, so I always worked two jobs. I
loved this about them; despite amassing more wealth than
they could have fathomed just a few years before, they did
not let it go to my head, they never wanted anything to feel
like it was too easily gained. And they always made sure I
knew how their wealth had been earned: from their very
blood, sweat and tears. From them I learned to keep my
head down, work hard, and always redouble my grit and
dedication to my pursuits. That if I was not succeeding at
something, it was because I was not trying hard enough.
That I always needed to do my best, and my best was perfec-
tion so nothing short of that would do. That not trying, not
accomplishing enough, would be to cop out, to fail to make
something out of all the privilege and opportunity they had
been able to give me, had wrung from their own exhaustion
and dedication. That to settle down with a great job and be
financially independent, able to support kids should I one
day choose to have them, was the pinnacle of accomplish-
ment, and the only way to show them how much I appreciated all they had done for me. That was the path I was on BTA,
and I had been happy with it. Happy to live up to their ex-
pectations, and my own. Happy that they never had to worry about me, not really. Happy my life was good and stable,
and I felt loved and supported and successful in the most
traditional sense. I liked it. I didn't want things to change or
be shaken up or turned upside down. And yet, here I am.
With nothing normal left.*

The next woman I spoke with was named Melissa. I am not sure if she told me that right away or later. She was incredibly calm and kind. More importantly, she knew what to do. I have no idea how she knew, or if she had been trained on situations like mine in the past, but I never wondered. I didn't have the capacity to wonder. She was not really a person to me, just a disembodied voice that knew all the things I did not. I did what she said to the best of my ability, because her confidence was the only antidote to my panic. She gave me very explicit directions which helped shake me out of my absolute inability to move. I had been frozen to the spot. She made sure my lights were off and my door was locked and dead bolted, then told me to barricade my door with any furniture I could physically move. I think I asked her what exactly I should use, but I don't recall her answer. I dragged my nightstand, reading chair, side table, suitcase and anything else I could get my hands on in front of my door. Then she told me to stay away from doors and windows and to go hide in my bathroom, with as many walls between me and the attackers as possible. She asked if the bathroom door also had a lock, and I said yes, and she said to make sure that was locked as well. It seemed genuinely ludicrous, because I had never before noticed how tiny and flimsy bathroom locks are in hotels, but I think I could have broken it with my bare hands if I had wanted. I desperately wanted to believe that some combination of what I had just done would keep those men out of my room, but knew it was completely futile. Reading chairs, nightstands and door locks are nothing compared to AK47s and grenades.

6 weeks ATA: I used to be a lot of things. I was a put-together person BTA. I had it all. Great job, amazing friends, kickass fiancé. I was climbing the corporate ladder with the best of them, and in my free time I was traveling the world and writing a novel. I volunteered at a preschool. I had a degree from a prestigious university. Today I am none of that. I still have some of those things, like amazing family and friends, but I don't feel that I deserve them. I can't work, I can't contribute, I can't power through this. I have always been able to power through anything. It's who I am. Or, who I was. But now I am weak. I look at my shattered psyche and I think, "Get over it." I have always just gotten over things. But not this. This taunts me. It leers at me, towering over me, and says, "You will never overcome this. You don't have what it takes. You are weak and pathetic. You should have died there." And I believe it. I wish desperately that the attack had never happened. That I could go back to my BTA life. But I can't. And I don't care about any of those things now. I don't remember how to kick ass and take names and climb the corporate ladder. I don't remember how to put my feelings aside and show other people that they come first. I don't even remember how to get a proper night's sleep or work out. So now I am in this purgatory, where I can remember what it was like to be a productive member of society, but I am unable to go be one. And the only skills I have, the skills to buckle down and grind, just aren't enough. I am not enough. This terrorist attack will kill me yet.

There was so much noise. That is hard to put into words as well. There was the suicide bomber, yes, and the immense noise of that initial explosion because it was so close. But the terrorists had also planted car bombs, which were going off and sending up massive plumes of smoke, the flames many feet tall. The explosions would set off car alarms as they exploded, so the sound of the bombs would reverberate, then linger, leaving the screaming of the car alarms in their wake. At some point, all the smoke caused the fire alarm inside the hotel to join the cacophony. It wailed above my head for some fifteen hours, screaming the terror I felt deep in my bones. For seventeen hours, the overwhelming stimulus of these sounds never let up. It made my nerves and brain scream like a prisoner of war being tortured, no sleep, no light, no ability to go outdoors, and all the while this infinite wailing noise, which alone is enough to drive you mad.

1 week ATA: Sometimes I just feel so overwhelmingly defeated. Like they took something from me that day that I can never get back. And I am tired of trying, just exhausted from the effort of beating my head against the wall, trying to regain my identity, to remember who I was before I watched them walk into my hotel, past the pieces of their former friend, without even looking down at the remnants of his body. Before I realized that some people, some human beings, have no regard for human life whatsoever. I try to remember what naive innocence felt like, what being happy go lucky felt like, what having a light and joyful heart felt like. But I can't remember. Those times are too far away now. I see them through a haze of new awareness; I can't empathize with how I used to feel, I can only shake my head at my own naïveté, and re-filter the memories through the new lens, thinking "Well, I am glad I lived through all of those things even though I was seeing the world through nonsensical, rose-colored glasses. That is a dangerous way to live when there is so much evil in the world. Never again."

I was entirely certain that I had mere minutes left to live. I accepted death, because I realized it was inevitable. My body went cold all over, and I was drained of energy. The best way I can describe it is to say I felt like I was already dead. So, I just crouched there, behind the bathroom door, and hoped they would kill me quickly. No part of me was left hoping that I would live, because I knew full well that I was going to die, we were all going to die, there was no one there to help us and we were unarmed, but just hoping it would be over quickly and I wasn't going to be taken or raped or tortured or filmed or beheaded. Those things seemed worse than death. My very last hope, my last living wish, was just to let my life end with a quick, single bullet between the eyes.

Every day for the first 5 weeks ATA: I have a flashback at least once per day. It's almost always that moment when I opened my curtains and saw the terrorists walking into the hotel. But when the flashback takes me by surprise, I try to take it by surprise in return. I imagine them dying a million different bloody, satisfying deaths right in front of me. Sometimes I kill them – I somehow have ninja stars or a machine gun or some other amazing piece of equipment that I use to end their reign of terror before it begins. Sometimes there is a Navy SEAL staying in a hotel room across the way and he takes them all out and I get to watch them bleed out with immense joy, my initial panic evaporating on the spot. Sometimes there is a hotel guard or Kenyan Special Forces guy on the roof, and he takes them out silently, sniper-style. I love to watch them die in my imagination, right there in front of me, in the courtyard, soaking up the blood of their exploded friend. I love to see my wish, that they would die and let us live, come true before they can inflict any more damage. And I feel a small voice in the back of my head reminding me that I don't advocate violence. Or do I? How did I used to think about these things BTA? I used to say things like, "Violence is not the answer to violence." Or, "Two wrongs don't make a right." I try to tell myself that I could just wish the men had been apprehended before they had shot anyone, instead of wishing they could die painful and bloody deaths in front of my eyes. But instead I just find myself wondering what I really believed before. I used to condemn violence publicly, sure, but if I am all the way honest with myself, wasn't there always another voice in the back of my head? One that used to ask, "What if they deserve it?" Or, "What would you have us do with people who rape and kill children? Spare them of violence? No way." But I never acknowledged it, not really mentally and certainly not verbally. But now something has changed in my brain. The voices have switched places. The one that used to sit quietly in the recesses of my psyche is louder, at the forefront. In fact, I can't hear the one that asks for mercy for criminals at all. I am not even sure it's still there. All I know is that at the end of the day, I don't wish that the terrorists had been apprehended alive. I wish I could have seen them die. And I know that if asked, I would have helped to kill them.

I decided to hide under the bottom shelf beneath the mirrored vanity, where I had crumpled all of my used towels. I don't know if Melissa suggested that I hide, or if I came up with it, but it was probably her. I pulled out the crushed towels and slid myself under that shelf, then pulled the towels back in front of me, desperately hoping I had properly covered every inch of my body, but not being sure. I tried and tried to tell myself it was an incredible hiding place, that if anyone walked in, they would never see me, and anyway, the terrorists would be in a hurry. So many people to kill. I could stay alive here. I thought very consciously about quieting my breathing, I didn't want them to hear me. I reminded myself over and over that I could not scream when they walked in. I had to be utterly silent. I would want to scream, every instinct would tell me to scream, but I could not. Screaming would mean the end of my life. I would give myself away to them if I did that. I bit down hard on my lips and waited – it was like the most gut-wrenching, high stakes game of hide and seek ever. Then it hit me: they would know I was in here. Someone had obviously barricaded the door from the inside. They would find me.

6 weeks ATA: I told my therapist once that some days I just want to crawl into a hole. But that's wrong. I'm in a deep, dark hole every single day, and some days I just can't crawl out. Some days the most immense hurdle I could possibly tackle is getting out of my bed and taking a shower. And on these days I feel so completely defeated, because now they've also beaten me mentally. The trauma is not over, it endures. The terrorists have followed me home and they torture me still, from beyond the grave. On those days I feel like I might as well just give up, because it's so clear that they have won.

I absolutely could not calm down; I could not process or think rationally at all. I am not sure if I had both phones at that time, or just the one I was talking to Melissa on. I believe I was barefoot, which would make sense. I can still feel that phone in my hand and see the dark shelf practically against my face. I can still feel the sense of urgency with which I hoped the hiding place would be good enough. I can still feel that hope die as the gunshots go on and on and on. I can still hear Melissa pleading with me to get ahold of myself and calm down, telling me that I am going to be ok. I can still jealously picture her safely at her desk, thankful that she is lying to me, but sad that I can't believe her. I can still see the image that hovered just behind my vision, embedded deeply in my own consciousness, of my parents receiving my body in a crude, wooden box. Their eyes would be downcast, they wouldn't want to look at this ruinous thing that had been their daughter but was now full of bullet holes. And they would be thinking exactly what I was thinking at that moment: that it had all been my fault. That I shouldn't have gone to Africa, but I had, and now I was dead because of it, and they had to live with the consequences. I hated myself. And I can still hear myself begging Melissa, desperately, to get someone to come help us. I think that's right. I think I kept saying 'us' not 'me.' I guess I was aware in the back of my mind that it was not just me in danger. It was not just me crying on my bathroom floor begging for my life. There were so many of us there that day. So many of us bonded in a horrible, twisted way, despite the fact that we would never meet, that we could not point one another out on the street. And so many, too, who would die.

Even rereading my own writing here feels insane. It's like

I have written yet another fiction, though for some reason the detail in this one is incredibly vivid, and the pit in my stomach as the letters blur by is so incredibly and acutely real. It's like the transcript of a movie that I know intimately, or a book that I have read before. Only the scenes are memories, and my heart races as I flip through the pages, because it didn't happen on my TV, it happened in my life.

I have to say, I prefer fiction.

Part Two:
Bank Robbery

A t some point while I was lying under that shelf, with my hips crushed in a way that would leave massive bruising, not feeling the pain of it thanks to the pure adrenaline my body was running on, Melissa told me it was a bank robbery. She said she had gotten word that it was a bank robbery gone wrong, and that the men who had tried to rob the bank were just trying to get away with the money, but that they weren't targeting the hotel specifically, that they weren't coming after me and the other guests. I believed her immediately, for two reasons: one, I remembered seeing a bank just outside the hotel in the little business plaza it faced. And two, because I so desperately wanted it to be true. I so desperately wanted those men to not be there to kill me. I texted my family that it was a bank robbery which meant I was considerably safer than I had previously thought. I think this is when I crawled out from under the shelf. There was no reason to hide from robbers who were trying to escape from the area. It was still very terrifying to be so close to gunshots, and I didn't fool myself all the way into thinking I was out of the woods, so I stayed huddled on the tile floor. One more explosion could bring the entire building down, one stray bullet could end my life in an instant. Or perhaps I didn't even delude myself that much, perhaps in the back of my head I knew this report was wrong. Perhaps I knew, as my dad would later text me, that 'a suicide bomber doesn't rob a bank.'

I never had panic attacks before. It feels like you go right back into full-on terror mode. You can't connect your thoughts. Your heart starts slamming and you hear it in your ears. You lose all ability to act or think rationally. You freeze in place, or perhaps fall to the ground because you can't breathe. Your chest is so tight, it feels like you'll never get your next breath. And in my case, I am completely sure the terrorists have found me. I feel just like I did on that bathroom floor. The first time it happened was 3 days ATA. Paul had washed the two shirts and one pair of pants I had made it out of Africa with. The pants were the ones I had worn all through the attack and then at the Embassy and on the planes all the way home. He brought the pants out of the laundry room and held them up, asking if they could go in the dryer or if they needed to air dry. I tried to answer but my words caught in my throat. I felt like I was going to throw up. My hands were shaking, and I was gasping for breath. My knees were buckling beneath me. I couldn't look away from the pattern on the pants, the pattern that I hadn't realized I had stared at for 17 hours while my life hung in the balance. I finally managed to whisper, "Get those away from me." Paul looked shocked, but as always, he reacted perfectly and instantly. As soon as the pants were out of my eyesight, I was able to calm down a little. Paul held me while I cried and tried to explain to him that somehow the pants had really upset me. He apologized but I told him it wasn't his fault. I just asked that he keep the pants far away from me.

The next time was about 8 weeks ATA when my apartment building was under construction, and the workers accidentally set off the fire alarm. I was in the middle of a meeting with the FBI when I started screaming. I tried to cover my ears, but I couldn't move. I fell down on the floor of our living room wailing, until Paul pulled me into the bedroom and shut the door, which muffled the noise considerably. The fire alarm turned off a moment later. I hadn't realized that having listened to a fire alarm for about 15 of the 17 hours of the attack, the sound would instantly take me right back there. The most recent and by far worst time was about 14 weeks ATA. A nearby college campus started setting off fireworks, I know now. Instantly, I could feel my brain tearing itself apart. I started shaking and crying and wailing and huddled into a ball on the couch. Paul kept trying to explain it had to just be fireworks, but we couldn't actually see them, only hear them, and my whole body wanted to just run, get away. I kept wanting to ask him if "they" were coming, not even knowing who that would be. I covered my ears, but I could still hear the sounds, and it was just like gunshots in the distance. I was absolutely convinced beyond all reason that they were indeed coming for me. Rationally, I knew it had to be fireworks; he was explaining how safe our location is, and even noted that if it was something dangerous, we would've heard sirens pretty quickly, which actually calmed me down a little. But I felt all the terror all over again. That horrible, deep despair of waiting for someone to come kill me. And no matter how much I tried to talk myself down, and no matter how frustrated Paul became (I think mostly with himself for *not being able to "help"), or how much he tried to explain, I simply couldn't calm down; I couldn't access any sort of rationality in my brain. I begged him, in sobs, for my noise-cancelling headphones when I could finally form a semi-coherent thought. I ended up turning on my audiobook as loud as it would go, which successfully eliminated the majority of the noise of the fireworks from reaching me, but I couldn't process anything that was being narrated; I was shaking and sobbing and hoping against all odds (it felt) that we would live. Paul was holding me fiercely, completely at a loss for how to help. Finally, he tapped me lightly and signaled that the noise was over. I asked him to look online for proof that it had been fireworks, and that the noise wouldn't start again. He found a local article confirming just that, and I finally calmed down a little. It was truly awful. We both sat there in silence, holding each other, shocked at how far from better I still was. Trauma recovery is a long, painful road. One that I could not traverse on my own. And it's ugly.*

I kept asking Melissa why. Why someone would want to do this. It was very hard to process because it was so incredibly senseless. It did not occur to me in those moments that so many times before I had seen terrorist attacks on the news and had simply shaken my head, sad at the state of the world, sad that people had died, but not really thinking deeply about the term terrorism, or the hows and whys of it. She didn't have an answer, of course, because no one really does. Instead she asked me to look around for something green. She told me that when she is really upset or anxious, she looks for something green. But there was nothing green that I could see in my bathroom. Everything was shades of gray or brown, accented with the hotel's accent color: orange. I asked her if it would be ok to look for orange things instead, and she told me that would be just fine. It calmed me down just enough that I could speak in a full sentence, which was pretty impressive at that moment. It calmed me down just enough to actually realize for the first time that my entire body – my legs, my arms, my core, my hands, everything – was shaking uncontrollably.

3 weeks ATA: Everyone needs me to tell them it's ok. To hug them and smile and say it's ok, I'm ok. Because that's what I do. That's who I am to all of these people. Or who I was. But I can't right now. I'm so weak, I have barely enough sanity and sleep to deal with my own thoughts and feelings, much less to carry their burdens. But I'm doing it anyway, best that I can. Because they need me to. And it's dragging me down, slowly but surely, deeper into the sticky, oozing mud of depression and lifelessness. I won't last long like this. I can't. But I don't tell them any of that. I just say, "It's ok. I'm ok."

It struck me suddenly that I needed to tell anyone I could think of in the area not to come near the hotel. I texted the people I was traveling with – thankfully, I knew they were out of the hotel at the moment, but I didn't want them trying to come back. My death would be enough, I didn't want anyone else to be in danger. I didn't want anyone else, anywhere, ever, to feel what I was feeling. To shake like I was shaking. To have to tell their families goodbye from afar, as I had done. To die on the floor of a bathroom, terrified, sobbing and alone. I texted my driver too, warning of the attack and telling him to stay away from the area. And it was with my driver, this man I had known for barely two days, that I shared my fear. I didn't want my parents or Paul or my brother to know how scared I really was. I didn't want them to think about me being afraid in the last moments of my life. It seemed a worse fate than death to have to be halfway around the world talking to your fiancé or only daughter, maybe for the last time, and unable to do anything. There is nothing worse for a parent than not being able to protect their child. I had to keep my chin up for them as best as I could. But I texted my driver and said: "I'm so scared." And I begged him, over and over, to send help. It seemed in those moments that somehow, with his local connections, he might be able to think of something. He might be able to contact the police chief or special forces, anyone, who might be able to help us. He was kind. He told me to stay calm, stay in my room, and that I would be ok. I realized he was just another person trying to tell me I would be ok, but ultimately, he had no idea; he was as helpless as I was. I stopped texting him. It was another sixteen hours before I realized he came to the hotel and waited all night, behind the police barrier that had been set up around the perimeter, to make sure I came out of there alive.

1.5 weeks ATA: Maybe for the first time in my life I truly empathize with the other side. I truly understand the fear that moves them. Part of me wants to agree, to say yes close the borders, ban Islam, and never look back. It is surreal, even now, to have these thoughts because I was always so adamantly against things like this, brushing off the people who said them as ignorant, not worth listening to, weak.

People who were moved by unfounded fear. I joined in a protest at Google when Trump passed Executive Order 13769, which he called Protecting the Nation from Foreign Terrorist Entry into the United States, but we called the Muslim Ban. I raged and cried and listened to stories of well-to-do, Google-employed immigrants who had been out of the country at the time, and then who had, using all of their privilege and first-world connections, barely made it back into the US after the EO had passed, and now knew so many who were stuck, unable to reenter this country that had, just a day before, been their home. I used to say very openly that ours is a country of immigrants, and to deny entry to immigrants would be to deny ourselves and our history, deny our very American-ness. But these darker thoughts appear openly in my own mind now, and they are indeed fueled by a deep, gnawing sense of fear. And the fear doesn't feel unfounded, or like it comes from a place of weakness. It's a fear that you can't tell who the good guys and bad guys are. Fear that in a day and age where even hotels aren't safe, how can we cling to idealistic beliefs? Fear that it's do or die time, literally. I think back on that executive order now, and how I used to feel that it was a thinly veiled move to further a racist agenda, but how now I am not sure it was such a terrible idea. If we don't know who the bad guys are, how do we keep them out? Perhaps broader measures are necessary. It's a complete reversal of anything I would have ever dreamed of saying before the attack, so I have more empathy for the other scared people who want to close the borders. I find myself wishing that I hadn't dismissed them, but had sat down with them, trying to understand their concerns. Trying to relate. Because we desperately need to converse, need to address the root issue. To put the fear in its rightful place, acknowledge it, then overcome it with logic. Today, I would tell the people I used to not understand that I consciously remind myself that there is danger here too. There are shootings here too. Anger here too. Closing the borders or any of the other "fixes" that are spawned from fear are a band aid on a bullet wound. Do we need to tighten up border security? Sure. Is that done through a wall between us and Mexico? Obviously not. Do we still need to welcome refugees and immigrants who are looking for sanctuary, looking for their own American Dream? I certainly think so. Which means we need better screening, better technology, and better wages for the people doing those jobs, not just a blanket ban on immigration from particular countries. I would tell them that we need to empathize, first with each other and then with the people who want to enter our country, because eradicating our fear and embracing empathy is the only thing that can reel in our division, internally and externally. The only thing that can truly save us.

Melissa was telling me that the police had arrived. The elation I felt was attenuated by the terror, but still there. Someone had come. Someone was trying to help us, trying to save us. I don't know if it's true, but suddenly I felt like I could hear a difference in the shooting. There would be a volley of insane, rapid-fire shots from what sounded like one side of the courtyard, then a pause, then a return volley, more organized and at a more regular pace, from the other. The return shots also sounded different, like they weren't just firing guns but also some large piece of artillery that made two sounds each time it went off. The new pattern of sound was more like a shootout, and less like a slaughter. I shook even harder than I had. Suddenly, there was a chance. Suddenly, it was possible I would not die. But in a way, that was harder. Being sure of anything, even death, felt easier to accept than being completely unsure. I was terrified to cling to the hope of life but was no longer completely resigned to death. I had entered into a painstaking limbo that would last sixteen more hours. Sixteen hours of wondering if maybe, just maybe, I might make it back out of the hotel alive. I hardly let myself acknowledge it. I needed to be brave, to go quietly, if someone still came to kill me. Hope was almost as harmful as fear to my sanity in those hours.

2 weeks ATA: I have a new sense of empathy for people with depression, people who have experienced trauma. I used to only observe it from a distance, curtly wondering in the back of my head how much of their pain was real, and how much was just self-inflicted. Wondering if they wouldn't be a lot better off if they just tried a bit harder, if they stopped leaning into to their sadness, if they were a little more like me. I learned, or thought I had learned, from my childhood that giving into pain, whether mental or physical, was a choice. But now I am like those people I used to judge, and I have a deep awareness of how impossible it is to just lean out of these feelings. Believe me, I have tried. Carolyn, my FBI Victims Specialist, tells me that on the plus side I can now connect with people who have experienced horrible things, that a simple look will pass between us and we will both know the other can understand, deeply and truly, what is happening within us. I do think that is nice because I believe in the power of empathy. But I am also acutely aware that to genuinely understand suffering is to suffer immensely, and that this empathy is costing me a part of my identity, a part of my happiness, a part of myself.

It wasn't long after that Melissa told me, "You've made it." I had been in the bathroom for just over an hour. I started sobbing so hard I couldn't get words out. She said she had gotten word that the hotel had been secured, and that Kenyan Special Forces were not only on the premises, but on the way to evacuate me. She told me they had a special password that they would yell when they knocked on my door so that I knew it was them. She told me to make sure I didn't have anything in my hands, or a backpack on, as there was still confusion about where all the bad guys were, so she didn't want any confusion with respect to me in particular. She told me to stay away from the door, as they would likely knock it down. She told me that they would have huge guns and flashlights, but not to be afraid because they were there to save me. I tried to tell her, through mangled sobs, how thankful I was. That I wasn't sure how much longer I could have lasted. That my nerves were completely frayed, and I just didn't have anything left. I didn't think I could spend another minute in there. But I didn't know then that I would have to spend over nine hundred more minutes on that bathroom floor.

3 weeks ATA: Carrie Underwood sings 'In the end, love wins.' I don't know that it's always true, but I will tell you this: ultimately, love (for your family, your friends, yourself) is the only thing that matters. And it's the only thing that will keep you going in the darkest of times. You have to remember that constantly, show it to yourself when you are struggling. I try to do that, always showing myself how much my parents love me, how happy and relieved they are that I lived. Same with Paul. Even though I am unbearable to be around these days. I remind myself of these things consciously, because it's my way of fighting back against the terrorists and their ultimate goal: to undermine my will to live even though I lived through the initial attack. To sow fear so deeply into my bones that the love in my life is drowned out. That's not to say I am winning the battle. The fear often does work that way, and on most days, I have to concede to them. But what keeps me going really, what keeps me from thinking about wanting to die all day long, is this conscious effort, this conscious reminder that there are so many who love me, and that in the end, their love will win out. Or at least, I sure as fuck hope so.

Melissa told me there was a car waiting for me outside, the last 4 digits on the license plate were 395M. I repeated that to myself a million times while I waited and waited for them to get to my door. She said she had booked a new flight for me to South Africa, so I could go see Paul as soon as possible. I couldn't even believe my ears. I was going to get out. I was going to see Paul again shortly. It all seemed impossible, surreal.

7 weeks ATA: I opened my work computer today for the first time since getting back. Two things caught my eye. The first was that I had received an email the day after the attack from what Google calls "People Ops" but most people just call HR. It was supposed to have 'support options' that were customized for my situation. Instead, when I opened it, I found a one-page Google Doc with my name misspelled, that said things like, "You can take five consecutive workdays off using sick time." Sick days? They were not serious. I was not sick with the flu; I was fucked in the head because of what I had seen while on a business trip for them! I felt like I had to be misunderstanding. The options were barely options at all, and certainly were not customized for my situation. They looked like they had been copied from some HR handbook and then pasted into a document that couldn't be for me, it didn't even have my correct name on it. And there was another email, this one also not for me, but about me. It was from Google's CEO, Sundar, and it told the entire company that one employee had been in that Nairobi attack that they had likely heard about in the news. No one had asked me if it was okay to share that, Sundar had not sent any sort of personal note to me whatsoever, but this email had gone out to the entire company; I had received it on BCC. At first, I felt nothing except for shock. This was a company where I had been happy for almost three years. A company that valued me as a person, not just an employee. A company that had kept me safe while I traveled the world on their business errands, until they hadn't.

Melissa asked if I had a small bag I could pack full of overnight supplies, as well as my passport. I told her I had a small backpack. She asked if I could get it ready, and I said yes, but once I had army crawled out to get it, shots still ringing outside my window, I couldn't think. I was crouching there, on the bathroom floor, staring at it. I upended it, so that it was empty, but then couldn't do anything else. My brain simply could not get to thoughts about being safe or having the option to take a shower or change my clothes. I was still in full-on fight or flight mode. Finally, I squeaked out a request to Melissa, "Can you tell me what to put in this?" Hero that she is, she told me exactly what to pack. I filled it with toiletries, a change of clothes, cash (which I hid in many different pockets, both in the backpack and on my person in case I needed to bribe different people at different points in order to get out of the country – that was not Melissa's suggestion but my own innovation), and my passport and personal documents so that I could get out of Kenya and into South Africa. She told me to put on thick-soled shoes, so I put on my tennis shoes. She asked if I had a jacket, which I did, so she told me to put that on as well. She told me KSF was almost to my door, so it was time to un-barricade it. She told me that when they got me, I shouldn't look around, I should just look at my feet, as I didn't need to be any more traumatized than I already was, and that the bad men had wreaked havoc and left a truly terrible scene in their wake. I barely processed that. All I could think was that I was getting out.

1 week ATA: Sometimes I can fake it for the people around me. I can slip back into the skin of my old self, the identity that is now dead to me. I stare at my phone and think: 'What would I have responded to this text a month ago?' Then I construct the text just that way, bit by bit. I add exclamation points that feel absurd and pretend to care about Instagram photos and parties. But it hurts me. It forces me to face the fact that I am not who I was. That I will never get that person back, that untroubled, successful, supportive person. She is dead, she died in the attack, and when I have to play her part it causes me to grieve her loss deeply, in a way that is profoundly personal. I have lost the person I used to know best, and I really loved that person, I was proud of that person. Now I am just an empty shell, a depressed, morbid piece of shit who didn't deserve to get out of there alive. I take up space in the world where genuinely helpful and wonderful people should get to exist instead. I am a waste of human life, who has lost all ability to feel or to contribute to society. I am alive, outwardly, but on the inside I am dead.

No one came. I sat by the bed, listening to the gunshots, which I was told were coming from the office park across the way (where the bank was located). I was told the bad men had holed up there and the police were still having a shootout with them, but that the hotel was perfectly safe to evacuate. Melissa would ask me every few minutes if I heard anything outside my door. I didn't. She would ask me if I could hear boots on the ground in the hallways, or people yelling, "Police!" I couldn't. She was as confused as I was that no one was showing up. Eventually, she called KSF, (how she had their number I have no idea) and patched them through so I could hear as well. The man who answered said his name was Peter, and he was on site at the hotel, helping coordinate the evacuation of the surviving innocent civilians. The connection was terrible, I could barely understand a single word, but Melissa said that he had said they were coming to get me. He confirmed my room number and said they would be there soon. They weren't. Melissa asked me a few minutes later to get up and look out my peephole. She said she got a report that they were right outside my door. They weren't. The hallway was empty. She asked me then if I was sure I had been saying the correct room number. Maybe that was it! I thought I'd had the room number right, but honestly everything at that point was so backwards that I wouldn't have been surprised if I'd had it wrong. I ran to the bathroom and started digging through the little trashcan, searching for my check-in paperwork. With each second that passed I was more and more sure that I must have given the wrong room number, that would explain everything! They were waiting outside a door, yelling the right password, it just wasn't my door because I had sent them to the wrong place! I just needed to find the correct room number, and then Melissa could get it sorted and they would come get me. I wrenched the little card holder they had given me at check in out of the trash and turned it over to see what room number was written on the back. But it was the same one I had been saying. So that was it. I was alone. If it wasn't the room number, maybe Melissa was just wrong, maybe no one was ever coming to save me.

5 weeks ATA: I went out for a friend's birthday today. She chose a busy restaurant in San Francisco. It was too much for me and I shouldn't have gone, but I am so fucking sick of the terrorist attack still stealing things away from me that I was set on being there. I couldn't track the conversation very well. The place was huge and loud, and we were seated upstairs which was way too far from an exit. I was constantly tracking the movement at the front door, waiting for bad men to come in and gun us down. The place would have made a great target: chock full of unarmed civilians but only one main entrance and/or exit. Block that with gunmen and you can kill us all at your own pace. Between these thoughts I would snap back into the conversation: ... something about Tahoe ... something about marriage. I felt guilty for not tracking better, but there was nothing I could do. My heart rate was through the roof. It wasn't a question of if people would try to come kill us, but when. Then everyone at the table ordered a drink. I did what I would have done BTA and asked for a glass of champagne. It was amazing. As I drank it, the hyper vigilance wore off. My heart rate came down and I felt considerably calmer. I forgot about the men coming to kill us. I participated in the conversation and even laughed at a couple of jokes. Then I realized what had changed. It was the alcohol. And even in the moment I realized why it's such a common story to hear that veterans suffering from PTSD spiral into alcoholism. It's incredibly comforting. It's the only thing that has made me feel normal since I got back. So, I have to draw a hard line in the sand to stay the hell away from this stuff until I am better. Because the spiral is never far off.

At some point, helicopters showed up. I think it was around this time. I told Melissa that I could hear helicopters and sirens, in addition to the alarms and gunshots and explosions. She said, "That's good!" and I believed her. I would take any support we could get; helicopters help fight bad guys, so it seemed good to have them there. What was strange was that they were hovering right outside my window. Their lights shined into the bathroom and lit up the floor all around me. It was startling. My brain started spinning out with questions: Why are they looking in the hotel? Don't they know the bad guys are in the office park? If they are looking for survivors, isn't it better to send people in to get us? Not peep at us from the cockpit of a helicopter. What the hell is going on? But I just hung on to the fact that Melissa said the helicopters were good. The helicopters are good. Then, I heard them. Not KSF, but the terrorists. Suddenly there was shooting, and screaming, and it was way too close. It was not out-side in the courtyard. I knew immediately that they were in the hotel. The sounds were coming from the direction of the elevator and stairs, and they were getting closer and closer to my floor. I started sobbing again, frantically asking Melissa if I should re-barricade my door. She said if I thought I was in danger then I absolutely should. I threw the furniture back in front of the door and crawled back to the bathroom as fast as I could. I was hunched, back on that tile floor, staring at my shaking hands. The gunshots crept closer and closer until they were on my floor. The noise was incredibly loud. The shots were accompanied by screaming men's voices, violently uttering words in a language I only recognized as not English. This was it. I had come full circle. I had accepted death, rejected it, thought I was getting out, but that had just been stupid and naive. I was never getting out. They were here, with their giant guns and their explosives, right outside my fucking door.

Every other week ATA: I wish I had a physical ailment so people could see how much I'm hurting. It would be so much easier for them to understand that way. They look at me and I look just as I did before, with only the slight difference of these dark circles under my eyes that tell the secret of my long hours of wakefulness each night. They are my night-mares, etched directly onto my face. But they are easy to ig-nore. People think I am a little tired, maybe, but otherwise fine. They want me to assure them that it is so. I want to scream in their faces that of course I am not fine, but anoth-er instinct wins out: silence. They can never understand, so why tell them anything? But as I sit there in silence, I think that if I just had a broken leg it would be so much easier. They would see the cast and think, 'Wow, that sucks. That must be really painful and inconvenient. There are so many things that she used to love that she can't do now. I hope she is getting better. I hope she is mentally and physically getting through this injury. A broken leg really sucks and it's a long journey.' Those are all the things I want them to think about PTSD, but it doesn't occur to them because there is no physical evidence that I am broken. No physical evidence that I am not fine, or that my injury might be very painful and inconvenient. That there are so many things I used to love doing but can't now. That it's incredibly tough on me mentally, and that it's a long journey. Instead we sit there, silently, across from one another and all I can think is that they must think I am milking it. I look fine, why can't I just act fine? No one ever thinks someone with a giant cast is milking it. But people can't seem to understand what they can't see.

The window blew out. Right by the stairs, on my floor, there was a massive sprawling window. It kept the stairs bathed in gorgeous natural light all day, and I had noticed its beauty more than once coming and going the previous couple of days. I heard it shatter. I knew exactly which window it was because of the truly extraordinary amount of noise it made as it crashed to the ground in a million pieces. That is how close they were. Literally around the corner from me. On the staircase I had passed just a few hours before. I couldn't breathe. I couldn't move. I couldn't think. I just sobbed and sobbed, thinking that I had really loved my life. That I wasn't ready to give up on it, but here I was about to die. That I had really, really wanted to marry Paul. And then as I listened, the noise moved away. They went further up the stairs, continuing their fire fight. I tried to focus on exactly what I was hearing, attempting to decipher the noises. It sounded like there was shooting from outside, and then returned fire from inside. I started convincing myself that the *good* guys must be inside, returning fire on the bad guys who had to still be outside. That was the only thing that made any sense at all. I could calm down a little, it wasn't the terrorists on my floor, they were holed up in the office park, right? But I think part of me always knew that good guys wouldn't sprint up the stairs of our hotel, putting the hotel guests in unnecessary danger and screaming at the top of their lungs. Part of me knew, even before I was told, that the terrorists were inside the hotel.

The things we own are absurd. They are meaningless and yet we constantly imbue them with meaning, desirous of making our hard-earned cash turn into something that helps us feel fulfilled. Little items we can own and fondle and keep close to us as symbols of who we are. Have your life hang in the balance, and suddenly every single thing you own will lose its meaning, instantly. Your things don't even occur to you, you forget that you own anything at all when death slams on your door. You want only to flee; you are an animal with no possessions. There is no price you can put on the laptop or bracelet or backpack that you would have to crawl past a glass window to get as gunshots explode just outside.

That was the next text I got. I was told the good guys were trying to sweep the hotel, but that they had 'encountered resistance' on the fifth floor. I was stunned. It was true, then, they were here. They were terrorists, not bank robbers, and they were inside my fucking hotel. The full-body terror, the utter loss of hope, had all returned in an instant. It was time, once again, to accept the inevitability of my death.

In the weeks after the attack, I did everything I could to erode my feeling of helplessness. I would never again be caught unawares in a dangerous situation because I simply hadn't done my due diligence. I would now be prepared for any situation at any time. I purchased mace and attached it to my key ring. Whenever I was walking to or from my car, I carried the mace in my hand, finger on the trigger. We installed a new security system and kept it on at all hours of the day, whether we were inside the house or away. I took jiu-jitsu and self-defense classes, learning how to get away from opponents twice my size. I felt ready for anything. But what I didn't realize, is that all of that preparation was predicated on the belief that the entire world is dangerous, and that the next tragedy was waiting around each and every corner to bulldoze me. It was a belief that had formed and then cemented in my brain during those seventeen hours of mental torture. And it was going to be incredibly difficult to change.

I had a glass water bottle that I had brought into the bathroom with me at some point. Perhaps it had been Melissa's idea to grab it. I wasn't very preoccupied with thirst, however, so I had all but forgotten it was there. Then, at some unexpected sound or explosion I turned quickly and accidentally knocked the bottle over, shattering it across the open floor of the shower. I yelped with fright, not having expected that sound either, and worrying for a split second that my window had blown out. Melissa asked me in a very urgent voice what the noise was, and I explained, shakily, that it was a broken bottle, that I had broken a bottle, and that for the moment I was ok. I waited, breathlessly, trying to listen for noise outside my hotel room door. Had the shattered glass attracted attention? Were the terrorists, even now, rushing for my door to find the idiot who had just shattered a bunch of glass? Had I alerted them of my location? Had I forfeited my life? After a few moments when no one had knocked down my door, I let my breath go, just hoping that no one had heard the bottle shatter over all of the other noise. I could still hear the gunshots and grenades just a couple of floors above me. I was safe, in that I was not yet dead, but I still knew my life would end in that hotel. They were too close, and I was too foolish, too clumsy. I would never make it out. I looked again at the broken glass, and there was only one thought, big and loud and flashing across my consciousness: broken glass makes a great weapon. Probably not in defending myself against terrorists armed with massive automatic weapons, but at least in choosing when and how my life would end. If I hid a particularly sharp piece of that glass in my pocket, then I could slit my wrists as soon as they broke my door down. I would rob them of my murder, and take back a tiny bit of control, and with it a tiny bit of dignity. I would insure against the possibility that they kidnapped or raped or tortured me. Death was death, and it would soon be knocking at my door. It seemed better to answer it myself than to let strangers deliver it.

How do you want to die? And I don't mean old and asleep in your bed. That's not an option. I mean if you had to choose between two absolutely abhorrent things. How would you choose? What criteria would you use? Would you pick whichever allowed you to have a longer life, regardless of how miserable that life was? Would you rather commit suicide or be tortured for the next several years? Would you rather jump out a window or burn to death inside a building? Would you rather take a single bullet to the head while facing your killers or be shot in the back running away? And what if these options were not hypothetical, but imminent? Can you really imagine what that would be like? I will tell you the answer: if you've never been in that situation, you can't. You might think a lot of brave or weighty things about death now, but all of those go out the window when you are really in the situation. When you are face to face with Death, you are pure terror, adrenaline and misery. You are soulless and alone. You are utterly and completely hopeless. You feel like you're already dead. That's how I felt on that bathroom floor. I was already dead.

Part Three:
Hostages

U nexpectedly, I got two great pieces of news. The first was that there were only five terrorists at most. My parents were quite sure – news had officially started to come out about the attack, as well as videos and photos, and the authorities were certain that there were only between four and five terrorists. I argued with them at first, for all the gunshots and explosions I had heard, it felt like there had to be dozens of these horrible men all around me. But they were steadfast. They had seen the pictures. There were only five, at most, and so with forces now on the ground to respond and secure the situation, five terrorists couldn't last too much longer. And then, the best news I could have ever hoped for: US and UK Special Operations Forces were officially on site. I couldn't help thinking: 'US and UK Special fucking Forces, the best in the world, are here?! They are going to help us?! Holy shit that is huge.' I texted this incredible news to my parents and Paul and we all shared in a single moment of celebration. A single moment where we could take one, uninhibited breath as we all thought the same thing: US and UK

Special Forces don't lose, right? Especially against only five terrorists! I told myself over and over that I have never heard of a story where we, the US Special Operations Forces, went into a situation like this and lost. Where we said, "Eh, fuck it. We will just let the terrorists have this one, they have a pretty solid foothold already." We don't quit, and we don't fucking negotiate with terrorists. We are America. It was the best piece of news I had gotten in five hours.

3 weeks ATA: Paul asked me today if I felt up to looking at a news story from the attack. I think he could see the struggle on my face: I didn't want to see anything remotely related to the attack, but I also didn't want to say no and disappoint him or seem scared, so I just hesitated. He jumped in and explained that it is a good story, and that nothing about it is scary, that he thought it might actually make me kind of happy. I agreed but was pretty panicked; I couldn't imagine any news stories that wouldn't make me feel terrified – I can't even watch news that isn't related to the attack. But I conceded because honestly, he is usually right. He read it to me, and it describes how a British special forces soldier (SAS) was shopping nearby when he heard the explosion. Instead of running for cover, he grabbed his tactical gear and rifle out of his trunk, put it on, and ran toward the attack. Ran into the hotel in fact and started pulling innocent people out. He was one of the first responders on the scene. That means he was totally alone, no team, no backup, no briefing. He just followed his gut, and his gut told him to go in there and save people. People like me. His gut told him to risk his life, off duty, to go save total fucking strangers.

I was wrecked. I just cried and cried, and couldn't put

any of it into words, but it was just so unbelievable that one lone guy would do that, risk everything for me and the others. I cried and I held Paul's phone and I zoomed in on the pictures of this guy that the internet is now calling Obi Wan Nairobi, which seems pretty fitting since he was our only hope, and I wished I could reach through the screen and hug him. Wished I could sob on his shoulder and thank him for what he did, what he saved, what he gave me and the world that day. Thank him for being the living proof that good can prevail over evil, that as much darkness as people can bring into the world, others can eradicate it with a single, amazing act. We tried to learn more about him, but there isn't much online, so instead we ordered a thermos that has the same logo that was on his backpack (Blackbeard's flag), and a patch that someone made in his honor, because I like to feel like I am keeping him close to me. I feel like if I have these talismans that are a direct connection to him then I will be safe. How could I not be if someone like that is nearby, if someone like that exists? I also just always want to remember that there are people like that out there, no matter how shitty and dark and scary this world gets sometimes. There are people like Obi Wan Nairobi who run toward the sound of a terrorist attack.

But that was all. Only one moment of relaxation and celebration before the next grenade exploded. And the next. And the next. Melissa told me to fill my bathtub with water in case the building caught fire all around me, as it would give me a temporary place to stay alive until, maybe, someone could come save me from the flames. I reminded her that the bathtub was right next to a massive window, which would have put me dangerously close to the whizzing bullets. She told me to wet some towels at the sink instead and surround myself with them. I was too afraid to turn on the water. She had told me so many times before not to make a single sound, and that much water felt like it would make a truly extraordinary amount of noise. I told her I wouldn't do it. But at the same time, I was thinking about how ironic it would be if, now that US and UK Special Operations personnel were there to save us, I burned to death, or the building collapsed and I died, crushed in the wreckage. I imagined that: them pulling the remnants of my body out of the mass of stones left behind by what was once a hotel full of guests and returning the pieces to my family. I screamed silently every time another grenade went off. I screamed and I covered my head and I hoped against hope that somehow, I would live.

3 weeks ATA: I am furious with religion and how it is per-verted for things like the killing of unarmed civilians. Is there anything more cowardly and less godly than that? I am furious with how we use religion to draw lines in the sand, to say we are different from one another, to go to war. I am not religious, and I haven't been for a long time, but I had never before seen, face-to-face, the infuriating way that it can be twisted, used as deception in a vicious effort to take inno-cent lives. On the flip side, though, through this experience I also saw, face-to-face, the beautiful things that can come from religion. I got so many texts on that bathroom floor saying that people were praying for me or thinking about me or hoping for the best. I didn't care what kind of language was used, I appreciated any and all good wishes, both dur-ing and after the attack. Isn't that what religion should be about? Supporting each other? Coming together? Just imagine what we could do if we all really did come together. We spend so much time tearing this world apart. We spend so much time creating misery for our fellow human beings or trying not to understand them. What if we spent the same amount of energy reaching across the goddamn aisle and saying: you're human, I'm human, we must have so much in common. Let's think about what we can do to make this world a better place. Together. We could find all the dark, empty holes where hate is bred. We could fill those places with love and understanding, with humanity and compassion. We could fight together, for the betterment of all mankind, instead of looking for differences, which only ever leads us to tear ourselves apart.

After Melissa gave me his number, I texted Peter from Kenyan Special Forces every so often to ask him for updates, as I didn't yet have a direct line to the US or UK Special Ops. He told me that evacuations were proceeding, but were often halted because, "The terrorists left booby traps for us everywhere." I closed the text window immediately when I saw that. A hotel full of booby traps and unidentified explosives was dangerous for everyone. Would Peter live? Would I? It wasn't until long after I was out that I learned that the people who were being evacuated were shot at by the terrorists as they hid inside the hotel. It wasn't until long afterward that I realized that even as I was longing desperately to be evacuated and handed off to US Special Operations Forces, the absolute best thing for me to do was stay exactly where I was. To continue to cower on the bathroom floor, and more importantly, continue to wait.

1 week ATA: Sometimes I feel great. It's not all bad. My life used to exist at a stable level of happiness and joy. People used to ask me how I was so happy all the time. I used to be aware that nothing terrible had ever really happened to me in my life, and to appreciate that immensely. I was not burdened, I had a beautiful, joyous life and used to wake up with a profound awareness of that. Now, my life has no equilibrium, no stability. I am either operating on a plane far above where I used to wake up, or I am slogging through quicksand far below. I am ecstatic or I am miserable, barely able to find the will to live. It oscillates at a moment's notice, giving me whiplash, and making me exhausted all the time, even in the happiest moments.

I experienced three extremely strange, almost out-of-body moments during the long wait. One was realizing that I should probably put my bra back on. It seemed odd and extremely low priority, but I had such a long time to wait, and it seemed almost rude to not be wearing a bra when/if people ever came to save me. And then the thought that it was rude nearly made me laugh out loud, which was extraordinarily bizarre, and thinking about how bizarre it was made me want to scream. I didn't even know if I would live, what the fuck did it matter if I was wearing a bra?! I wondered about it on and off for about an hour before I finally just put the bra back on, if for no other reason than to quash that particular series of thoughts.

The second strange thing I experienced was more of an utter break with reality. My brain was spinning so hard trying to come up with some sort of explanation that would mean that I was safe and that I would make it back to my family, that finally I landed on one that was truly bizarre: that I was in some sort of fucked up show. The Truman Show was one of my favorite movies as a kid, and so I started wondering if it was possible that, like Truman, I was simply at the center of some elaborate show, and the terrorist attack was a plot line intended to stir up viewer interest. It almost made sense; sitting in the middle of a terrorist attack was so insane, so hard to relate to even as I was living it, that it almost felt like it had to be fake, or maybe I just desperately wished it was. I started rocking back and forth as I sat on the floor, trying to convince myself that I was indeed living inside of a constructed, TV show world, and repeating to myself over and over: 'They never kill the main character.'

The last was the overwhelming need to pee. It's funny how your brain can feel your body knocking. How you swat away your biological desires like flies, and most of them recede entirely: you feel no hunger, no thirst, no tiredness, which allows you to channel all focus and energy toward survival. But the need to pee, that doesn't go away. It continues to nag at your consciousness, and when swatted away it simply returns, more aggravated, until you hit a point where you absolutely cannot ignore it. I had to pee so badly, and I was right there next to a toilet, but I was so afraid of making noise that I fought it for a really long time. Then when I could fight it no more, I went over to the toilet to pee. Have you ever tried to pee while shaking and sobbing uncontrollably? It's very difficult. It almost made me want to laugh, if the laugh hadn't been stifled by my tears and terror.

You learn to make jokes about what happened. Really

terrible, dark jokes. I found myself saying things like, "Oh, well you know what they say, naps will kill you!" Or: "Why don't we get an Airbnb? I have heard hotels can be really dangerous!" Or: "Sure, let's plan our honeymoon! I am down for anywhere but Africa!" All of these are followed by a stiff laugh. But that laugh never sounds quite right. It's hiding too much. It's hiding fear and discomfort and your new-found inability to fit in or relate to the culture around you. But more importantly, it's hiding your tears. You can choose to cry about what has happened, or you can choose to laugh. Both are oddly painful. But at least when you choose to laugh, the people around you laugh too. Their laughter also rings too hollow, they too recognize the macabre nature of the jokes, which inherently makes them uncomfortable. But it's better than crying, because at least it keeps them from looking at you with that deep pity. At least it keeps them from looking at you like a broken doll that may never be pieced back together. So, you laugh that dark, false laugh, and you make jokes. Because it's the lesser of the evils.

Let me tell you about the state of the hotel during the attack. Strangely, I had electricity and Wi-Fi the entire time, which was absolutely critical to me staying connected with my family and with the security teams. That was an invaluable stroke of luck. As I have mentioned, the fire alarm went off for most of the seventeen hours. I barely noticed it, until at some point maybe halfway through it turned off. Suddenly, the wailing in my ears died, and in it dying I noticed how nice it was to have it gone. It was a temporary comfort. There were too many bombs, too much smoke. It came back on a couple of hours later and was on for the remainder of my time there. I don't remember hearing it when I was evacuated, but it must have still been on. I was so used to it by then. It was the pulse of my heartbeat, and the screams I couldn't utter. At different points, I could hear furniture moving loudly, scraping across the floor, perhaps above me or in the hallway outside? Or both at different times? It was startling, because it reminded me of all the other helpless victims inside the hotel who were just like me. I wondered if they were barricading their doors or trying to escape. I wondered if they, too, were alone. I wondered if I could join them. But these were quick thoughts, flitting across my consciousness and then gone again in an instant as my brain refocused on self-preservation, on survival. There was no room anywhere in my brain for anyone else in the hotel, horrible though that is. Every few hours, I would hear men's voices screaming, with the noise always seeming to come from a different direction. Early on, I thought I heard boots tromping around, and voices yelling, "Police!" I am not sure though, as that may have just been wishful thinking. Later, it was the men screaming as they came up the stairs. Later still, I thought I could hear screaming voices through my ceiling, which must have been the terrorists on the fifth floor, recognizing that they were cornered, trapped. How the tables had turned. But those were the only screams, I never heard the screams of the other victims, the hostages, the innocents. I guess that shows you who the truly brave ones were that day, and who the truly cowardly ones were as well.

First 4 weeks ATA: *One of the worst things the attack did to me is made it so I can't read. I can't focus for long periods of time. I lose my train of thought constantly when trying to converse. I can't follow in-depth conversations or listen to audiobooks for very long. I am tired all the time, and my brain flits from topic to topic without my consent. I used to know how to find solace in books. I used to know how to use them to escape to another world. But the shattered pieces of my brain and consciousness won't allow me to do so now. It's torture. All I can do is watch TV. Like a vegetable, for hours upon hours I sit there, watching whatever idiocy comes on. Reality shows are particularly comforting. They take almost no brain power to watch, and the plots are so shallow that even if I fail to track them properly, I can still follow the show overall. I never used to watch TV like this. Maybe once or twice a year if I was too sick to go out and felt foggy, but not like this for days on end. I can't even get up to fix myself food. My parents take care of everything. I feel almost like I am in a coma. Am I even here?*

Paul told me I had to call the Embassy. I didn't want to hang up with the Google security team, so I was pressing him, asking why I needed to do that and was it really necessary. He grew stern, and it was the only time in the whole seventeen hours that he seemed frustrated with me. He told me it was of the utmost importance, and that I needed to get in touch with them immediately. He said they had been trying to track me down, but hadn't been able to get through to me, so they had gotten his contact information somehow and demanded that he get me to call them. They told Paul there was information they needed to get from me directly, and that no one else could provide it on my behalf. Paul told me they were expecting my call, and I needed to hang up with the security team at that instant and talk to the Embassy. He provided the number. My hands shook as I ended the call with the security team. It was absolutely disheartening to be completely alone, as I felt in the instant that I hung up the call that had lasted for so many hours. There was no one in my ear telling me I would be ok, true or otherwise, and it was stark and upsetting. I called the number Paul gave me, and it was answered quickly by a severe and hurried man's voice. He told me I had reached Marine Post One. I tried to explain who and where I was, and he quickly put it together. He had my name and wanted me to confirm my room number, which I did. He asked me, repeatedly, whether I knew of any other Americans in the hotel. I racked my brain but the only other American I was traveling with was not in the hotel, and I knew that for a fact as she had responded to my text telling her not to return. I tried desperately to think if I had overheard any American accents at mealtimes or in hallways over the previous two days, but my brain was fried; I couldn't think of anything. I began to worry that by forgetting someone I may have passed for a mere moment, I was now endangering their life. I started to cry at my uselessness, but the man on the phone was brisk. I could hear other phones ringing, other voices in the background. I could tell he needed to get off the phone and take care of other responsibilities. He told me one last thing: that our people, American forces, were going to get me. By this point, however, I was so skeptical that I repeatedly asked him to reaffirm what he had just said. He assured me that the good guys were indeed coming, and that all I had to do was sit tight for a little longer.

I had never before had the urge to break things. I mean, maybe, in a moment of frustration, but I wouldn't have real-

ly done it. ATA, I wanted to break things for weeks on end. Anything. Anything that would smash all to bits and give me the satisfaction of having completely decimated something. To inflict the inner ruin I was feeling on something external. To make a piece of glass look the way I felt. I asked around constantly trying to find out if there was a business that allowed people to come in and smash things. I fought the urge to break knick-knacks around my house with great difficulty. None of the things mattered anyway, and if smashing them was going to give me some sort of catharsis, why not smash them? But what I remember most is when the desire to smash things finally ebbed. When I could pass the little glass frame next to my bed and not want to destroy it. Because it was like a weight had been lifted off my chest. A weight that had caused me to want to smash things in my struggle to get free. I could finally breathe again.

I had spent so many hours on my bathroom floor that both phones were dying. The panic was intense because there were no plugs that fit my adaptor in the bathroom, just an oddly shaped one that only worked with the hotel-provided hair dryer. I told Melissa that the phones were dying, and I could only charge them in the bedroom. We both searched our minds for a solution that didn't send me into the room where one entire wall was basically glass. I was struck with a genius idea: I had a portable power bank in my backpack! I always carried one on international trips, just in case I ever ran out of power while I was on the go and needed a phone to work, but this was a far more useful scenario. It could literally save my life. I pulled it out of one of the pockets of the backpack that I hadn't emptied hours before, and, exultant, plugged it into my personal phone. Nothing happened. Confused, I hit the power button repeatedly, but still nothing. I shook it, I flipped it over, I tried everything I could think of, legitimate or otherwise, to get it to turn on, but nothing worked. It was completely dead, worse off than either of my phones. That was that, then. My chargers were with me, and I felt I had no choice. The one thing I could not do was lose contact. I had to army crawl into the next room, get to the nearest plug and get one of the phones charging at least. I started a ridiculous game of musical phones, where I would talk on one until it had only a few percent of its charge left, give myself a pep talk until I had the requisite bravery cached to army crawl back into the room of glass, swap the phones, army crawl back into the bathroom, and then call the security number back and tell my family to switch the number they were texting. This went on for over ten hours. Soon, it was not Melissa on the phone anymore, but CeCe, then Cole. They only do 8-hour shifts, so I talked to three people in my seventeen hours. I shuffled my phones god knows how many times. But the phones were my lifeline. The people on the phones reminded me, constantly, that no matter how much I wanted to, I couldn't run. I had to stay put. The people on the phones reminded me that I had a home and it was safe and I might just make it back there one day. The people on the phones were my reason to live.

2 days ATA: I still marvel at how easy it is to charge a phone here. Pop – you just snap it right in, it's so handy. Once you've had to army crawl across your hotel room floor to stay below the window level, as you cry and cringe and shake at the explosions just outside your room, wishing des-

perately that you believed in a god, any god, so that you could pray to him or her and beg that a stray bullet not blow out your window and kill you at that instant, because you really would like to charge your phone so that you can keep updating your family and, if necessary, tell them a final goodbye, you'll never again feel the same about charging your phone. Pop!

The next news I received was perhaps the worst of all. Worse than the fact that these men were not bank robbers but terrorists. Worse than the fact that they were inside the hotel. I received word that they were not just inside and on the fifth floor, but that they had taken hostages. It was not beyond me, even through the terror and adrenaline, to feel empathy. My sobs redoubled, I let my face rest against the cool, tile floor while I cried and cried for those people, just two floors above me, who were being held at gun point by these men. Men who wanted to kill them. Men who were likely screaming in a foreign language, wielding weapons and tossing grenades. If I was being held by the terrorists, I would probably, quite literally, drop dead of fear. As it was, my heart felt like it was going to explode out of my chest, bursting in an instant, and leaving my lifeless body in its wake. But if I had been up there, on the fifth floor, I don't think I would have made it. A little piece of me died when I heard that news that I will never get back. A little piece of my heart went with those hostages and left a dead space in my chest that I will never fill. Apparently, the terrorists were trying to make it up to the top floor of the hotel and trying to use the hostages to negotiate. The sounds that were above me took on an entirely new meaning. We were all, more or less, being held hostage, but I just couldn't imagine the terror gripping the hearts of the people unlucky enough to have been physically taken by the terrorists. And I couldn't ignore the thought that was screaming inside my brain: that it could, so easily, have been me. It still could be me.

1 week ATA: I am standing there, letting the hot water run down my back. Like I so often am now, I am there but also not there. I can feel the hot water, and it's soothing and nice, but my brain is somewhere else. I don't even realize where until my knees buckle. I hit the floor of the shower and I am already sobbing. I curl into a ball as I see them: the duffel bags. The day before the attack, I was in the hotel gym. I was on a spin bike at about five in the morning because of the jet lag, and a man got off the elevator (which opens directly into the gym) with a big duffel bag. I tried to smile at him as he walked by me to get to the locker room, but he just looked at the ground. That felt strange to me; it seemed customary for everyone in Kenya to greet others with big smiles. A few minutes later, a woman got off the elevator with a big pink duffel bag. She also refused to make eye contact with me as she walked by me to get to the locker room. I remember also thinking it was strange that they were not in hotel uniforms, but they were not in workout clothes either. And for the next twenty minutes that I was there working out, neither of them came back out to start their work out. It was all odd. But it was five in the morning and I was jet lagged as hell. I forgot about it and took a photo out the window of the gym to show my parents. It looked just like so many other big cities I had been to, all around the world. With the gray of the morning, it reminded me of Hamburg in particular. My parents were so silly and so prejudiced to worry about me coming to Africa. Nairobi was so safe. They were being ridiculous. Except that they were right. And now, shaking and sobbing uncontrollably at the bottom of my shower, I wonder what the hell was in those duffel bags. There were reports that the terrorists had been able to stash additional weapons and ammunition inside the hotel in the days before the attack. There were also reports that during the attack, they were trying to make it up to the top floor of the hotel: the gym. Did I watch people stock weapons in the gym for our execution and not even realize it? Is there something I could have done? I lie there, forgetting the hot water, seeing nothing but duffel bags, feeling nothing but terror.

Once again, no one came. It wasn't surprising any more. The Kenyan Special Forces hadn't come to get me when they said they would, the US Special Ops guys hadn't come to get me when they said they would. I thought the same thing that I had for so many hours: maybe no one would ever come. These few terrorists must really be putting up one hell of a fight. The explosions and gunfire I could hear through my ceiling certainly seemed to imply it was so. When I couldn't stand the wait any longer, I called Marine Post One back. Again, the man who answered was gruff and rushed. He told me in a few concise words that the plan had changed. American forces would still come to get me, he said, but that it would be a while. They first had to 'eliminate the threat.' It sounded legitimate; I didn't particularly want to flee a hotel full of living terrorists, accompanied by US Forces or otherwise. What struck me was that there was no estimate of how long that would take. Marine Post One didn't have an answer regarding the duration of the new plan. He told me it might be a long time. He didn't have any comforting words, or reassurances either. He was in a hurry, with a lot to take care of. He wasn't there to hold my hand, and I understood that, but it was scary and, in a way, disappointing. Once again, hope felt like it had been snatched away from me. Once again, I was staring at the dismal possibilities of the building exploding and me and my body being crushed by the wreckage, or a stray bullet flying through my window and ending my life. Once again I was faced with an indefinite sentence, and told that it was imperative that I didn't leave my room, which of course, was the worst thing to hear when all I had wanted for over seven hours was to get the fuck out of there. It was like a living nightmare that wouldn't end. Hope and salvation were dangled in front of me every so often only to be snatched away. I started to wonder if I might lose my mind there, even if I didn't die. Once again, I took off my backpack since no one was coming. I slumped down against the wall and did the only thing I had been able to do for so many hours. I waited.

9 weeks ATA: My therapist told me a great metaphor today. She told me that it's not unusual that I often feel out of control of my emotions. She asked if I felt irritable, if I was yelling at loved ones, and then afterward feeling very guilty. I told her that was exactly what was happening. She told me that's completely normal. (That is the best thing about trauma therapy. For that hour, everything I say is 'normal.') She told me that I am like a reservoir. I can hold up to a certain amount of water, but let's liken the water capacity to my emotional tolerance. Usually, I have a ton of capacity. My water level is low, and when little things happen, they add a little water to the reservoir, but it's far from spilling over. The terrorist attack filled up the whole damn reservoir. Which means that tiny additional drops simply make it overflow. I have no excess capacity. Slowly, she and I will work to drain the water left over from the attack. She said it's hard but rewarding work. And that will help give me back some capacity. So that instead of having a six-hour meltdown when I see something that reminds me of being in the hotel that day, I can recenter, and let it roll off my back. I really hope she is right. I need to believe that she is.

Someone knocked on my door! It sounded like they tried to get in, shaking the door handle, and then ringing my doorbell. I felt like I had been struck by a bolt of lightning. It was terror and joy all at once, because I couldn't be sure which to feel. Was it the bad guys or the good guys? I whispered to whoever was on the phone with me by this point, I can't remember if it was Melissa or CeCe or Cole, that someone was knocking. They cautioned me not to move, not to make a single sound, until the people at the door identified themselves. They reminded me that Kenyan Special Forces had a special password they would announce, and so if they didn't say anything, they could not be Kenyan Special Forces. I sat there, in my bathroom, night falling around me, holding my breath. They moved on to the next door, and I could hear them knock on it and ring the bell. Hope was still lost. To this day, I don't know who that was, or whether their intentions were good or evil. But I think about it all the time and wonder what would have happened if I had opened my door.

A moment in the life of someone with PTSD: "...So anyway, now he moved back, and it's so great because..." Holy shit, this restaurant is so easily accessible! Don't they care about security at all? They could at least have a couple of guards, I mean, who knows who could walk in off the street, you can't trust anyone these days. There aren't even metal detectors, which means people could already be in here with weapons! That means any second bad men will pull out guns and they will make us crawl under the tables and hide, and I wonder if they would think to check the bathroom, I guess at the first sound of a gunshot I will crawl under the tables and sprint toward the bathroom. Women's restrooms usually lock from the inside, so maybe I would be safe there. Unless they wanted to shoot the lock, which would probably open the door, and... "Meyli? Did you hear me? I was asking if you're free on Saturday. We all want to have dinner!" "Oh, umm, Saturday, I umm, I probably am, I can check, hang on." My calendar, my calendar on my phone, I need to check my calendar, am I free on Saturday? Or Sunday? What did she say? Jesus, my hands are shaking, it's hard to use my phone. I wonder if we will even live to see Saturday, with this restaurant being so goddamn unprotected. But the bathroom, yes that's right I was thinking maybe I could be safe in there. Maybe I can lock it from the inside and then find a hiding place, I am good at hiding, and then even if they do shoot the lock and come in, they won't find me. Or maybe there is a window in the bathroom, and I can crawl out of it and get to safety and actually escape, and oh my god what the hell was that?! Oh, I think it was just a broken dish. Christ, I hate the sound of breaking glass, oh my fuck. Never again, I am never going to a restaurant again, I can make better food at home and it'll save me the damn heart attack, and... "Meyli? Earth to Meyli! Are you checking your cal or are you like distracted on Instagram? Can you make it Saturday or not?" "Oh, sure yes, Saturday. Yeah, sure. I will be there."

I was terrified as night fell. For some reason we believe that the worst things go bump in the night. These terrorists had showed up in broad goddamn daylight, but still, somehow the night was even scarier. I wasn't allowed to turn on my lights as that could alert the bad guys of my position, so the bathroom grew darker and darker around me. Occasionally the room lit up as a helicopter would pass and its lights would shine in my window, but mostly I sat there in complete darkness, seeing only the background light on the screen of my phone. The terror gripped me then in a new way. The ever-present explosions and gunshots felt closer, scarier. It felt like someone could be hiding in my closet or bathtub and I wouldn't even know it. Like there were new terrors that I didn't even understand or anticipate yet. It also just seemed certain that if the good guys weren't able to win while the sun was still up, they were sure to lose now that it was dark. Upstairs, they were trying to fight back against evil, but darkness welcomes evil. The night was sure to take the side of the bad guys, and we were all doomed. Doomed to die alone, in the dark, on the far side of the planet in our hotel rooms.

We are evolutionary creatures. Fear etches into our brains more strongly than other emotions and we relive how and why we ended up in a scary situation over and over, trying to find the key to never ending up there again. That is why the terrorist attack didn't end when I finally was able to leave the hotel that day. That is why it didn't end when I got back to the US, or saw my family, or even got back to my apartment in California weeks later. It still hasn't ended for me. Because my brain now sees danger everywhere. I re-trained its neural networks in a way that says that what I once believed is safe, is not. And more painfully perhaps, I believe it is my fault. I believe that if I had been smarter, or more prepared, or more responsible, I wouldn't have been in the hotel that day. I wouldn't have spent 17 hours cowering on my bathroom floor. I wouldn't have put my family through 17 hours of torture while they were unsure if I would live or die. Unsure if each text they saw from me was the last. I lie awake at night thinking that their pain, my pain, all of it, is my fault. And my brain searches desperately for a way to prevent anything like that from ever happening to me or my family again. But it returns no guaranteed solutions, so it just spins and spins and spins while sleep evades me. That is what I work on with my therapist. She says it wasn't my fault. I am working really hard to try to believe her, but it really is like trying to re-retrain my brain. It's very difficult. But ultimately, she's right. I think.

Have you ever actually wished someone would die? Genuinely drop dead, never to return to this planet? I don't mean you wished for a moment that someone you were mad at would die, like the girl at school who was mean to you, or a parent who pissed you off. I mean, if it were up to you, you would genuinely end that person's life forever. I had never wished that before, not really, and it changes you. I never had really believed that I could feel that way, that I could genuinely wish another human would die. I was always the person arguing that no one was beyond saving, that there is good in everyone, that we have to slow down, be less judgmental and try to help each other instead of trying to destroy each other. But that night, as I sat on the floor of my bathroom, that is the thing I thought the most. I wished, with all my heart, with every shred of my being, that those men would die. Because their death was the only assurance of our freedom, and the freedom of the hundreds of innocents inside the hotel was well worth the deaths of those five men. I had finally found a situation where I felt that some people were truly beyond saving.

1 week ATA: My brother, Max, told me about cognitive structures today. He said he read up on PTSD, and learned that it's caused by the decimation of our cognitive structures. Over our lifetimes, we build up these beliefs, which are supported by our experiences and observations, like: hotels are safe. Or, people are generally good. But then, in these instances of massive trauma, those 'cognitive structures' or systems of belief are destroyed in a single stroke. They leave us in a wasteland, looking around at all the things we thought were true and scratching our heads, saying, "Well what the fuck actually is true then?!" And rebuilding those structures, in whatever new form the beliefs will take, is incredibly difficult. It takes a ton of work, it typically takes years, but trauma survivors have to try to rebuild them in weeks, or months. That is a big part of why PTSD saps so much energy.

Some of the cognitive structures that were destroyed for me that day are as follows: People are inherently good. I would not kill anyone. International travel is not generally

dangerous. Empathy can solve anything. I am brave, respon-
sible, and independent. I am safe. I know what matters in my
life. I will live a long and happy life.

Imagine trying to get back to your life, trying to confront
a single day, when none of that feels true anymore. When
you don't know what to believe, or whom to trust, or where
danger might lurk. It feels absolutely fucking impossible.

These are actual texts I received from total strangers
during the attack. I have omitted names to be polite:

"Meyli my name is –. I'm a producer with ABC News. I
hope you are safe. I'm trying to reach Americans who are
in the hotel for an interview. Are you available to speak to
me? Again praying for your safety."

"Hi Meyli,

My name is – and I work for Good Morning America on
ABC. Our thoughts and prayers are with you during this
incredibly difficult time and we are hoping and praying
you are safe.

I'm so sorry for bothering you. I just wanted to see if it
would be possible to give me a quick call once you are
safe.

We are so sorry about everything that has transpired
and hoping you and everyone with you is okay.

All my best,

–"

Needless to say, I didn't respond.

What is interesting about tragedy is what you see in re-
sponse. I have been shocked by who has reached out, as well

as who has not. I have been amazed by kindness and compassion from total strangers, as well as a complete lack thereof. A few days ATA I called United, trying to inform them that I would not be using the rest of my international travel itinerary, as I was already back in the US due to an emergency. I didn't want to get into the details as I was worried I wouldn't have the strength to do so. I asked the man on the phone if he could cancel my itinerary without all the fees, given that it was a legitimate emergency. He said he could not. I asked to talk to his supervisor, a young woman who apparently was having a hell of a day. She screamed at me until I quite literally cried, that she absolutely would not waive any fees, as this was a 'voluntary' change, regardless of the circumstances. I told her, through my tears, that I was in a terrorist attack and requested that she not use the word 'voluntary' anymore. With an edge in her voice, she told me that no matter what she called it, she was not going to waive any fees. I hung up. I called back later and saw the absolute flip side of humanity. A kind older woman named Diane answered. She told me there was a note in my file from the earlier supervisor saying no one was allowed to waive any fees for me, but that she would talk to her own supervisor and argue my case. She listened to what had happened to me and told me how sorry she was. She successfully advocated my case and waived all the fees. I cried again, but this time it was tears of joy. It was funny, such a small thing, but a perfect example of the difference a little kindness can make, even from a stranger. And I have had so much kindness since I got back: housing with friends, love and support from family and colleagues, and so much more. But we have also seen the darker side with people who haven't reached out or don't much care about what happened, landlords who are numb to our pleas about needing to move to a building that is not under construction, and others. If I have learned one thing, it's just to treat everyone you meet with kindness. You don't know anything about them or what they are going through. And you just might be the stranger who completely changes their day. You might be their Diane on a day that was otherwise filled with tears and misery. As Ellen says, be kind to one another.

I had been reiterating information on several text threads for most of the attack. I would type an update to Paul, then copy and paste it to my dad, then to my mom, then start over. Fairly quickly, my parents consolidated their thread, but I still kept theirs separate from Paul's. With Paul, I could ask him things like, "Do you really think I will live through this?" With my parents I tried to keep things lighter, less scary. I didn't want them to know that I had lost all hope. I didn't want them to know that every few seconds when I heard a gunshot or explosion I still nearly jumped out of my skin. I didn't want them to know how much I had cried, or how scared I really was. But Paul never lies to me. It's our promise to each other. So I could have these more open moments with him, and I knew he would tell me how much danger he genuinely believed I was in. My parents would have just told me I would be fine, because that is what they needed to believe.

15 weeks ATA: The guilt is what kills me, what gnaws at me relentlessly throughout the day and keeps me from sleeping at night. The guilt for what I put my family through for 17 hours. And what they are still going through today.

Everyone asks me if I am ok. But what about them?! I was just stuck. There was nowhere for me to go and based on random chance (until spec ops arrived) I was either going to live or die. I lived. But my parents, Paul, these incredible people who have vowed to protect me, were completely im-mobilized. Rendered completely impotent by distance and time zones. They had to live their worst nightmare for 17 hours, not knowing if I would live or die. They too are haunted by PTSD and nightmares, only they don't have ther-apists, and no one remembers to ask them how they are do-ing. They too are still fighting the battle against what hap-pened that day, they too have a new and darker lens through which they see the world. They worry about me now more than ever, and when I travel or fail to answer their calls or texts in a timely manner, they are forced to relive the terror of those hours. I don't want them or their pain to be forgot-ten. So I carry their torches too; I think of them constantly. And it kills me inside because I really do feel that it's my fault. I talked to my therapist about this today, and she brought me the first respite I have felt on this topic for months. She asked if I was sure I was going to die in those first moments after the initial explosion. I was. She asked what I would have done if I was going to die for complete certain. I said I would have texted my family goodbye and told them I love them, which I did. She asked, then, how I can feel guilty. She said I did exactly what I should have done in that situation, and that I cannot hold myself respon-sible for what the terrorists put us all through, that day and every day since. I know it sounds so simple, and like I should have realized it myself, but until she said it to me today, I couldn't see the logic through the guilt. It has lightened my load, at least for today. But I can still feel the guilt there, lurking at the edge of my periphery, waiting for its moment to sneak back in and crush me.

Eventually, all that copying and pasting and trying to track where I was in each conversation while switching which phone was charging became incredibly tedious. There was a single moment where I decided that I could not copy and paste a single additional text. I was so low on energy I could barely think or function. I asked my parents to please add Paul to our thread so that I didn't have to swap back and forth anymore, and they did. But that prompted my mom to say she also wanted to add my brother. I could have screamed. I wanted so badly to stop her from doing so, but before I could even respond, she had added him. It was awful. It broke my heart. I could still die at any second, and I had purposely not reached out to my brother the whole time. The kid is eighteen. He has his whole life ahead of him. He did not need to hear play-by-play updates of explosions and gunshots while his sister sat in a hotel room halfway across the world hiding from terrorists. His last memory of me was supposed to be just two weeks before that, when I was in Ohio playing Settlers of Catan with him. He was supposed to remember giving me a terrible beating at the game and staying up late watching TV and talking about life, love and philosophy. He shouldn't have been exposed to the gruesome reality inside the hotel, wiping out any beautiful final memories he had with me and replacing them with these snippets of conversation back and forth, "Have you heard anything lately?" "More explosions. I love you all." But I was too exhausted to be furious. I could only feel a deep, soul-crushing depression that the one person I couldn't stand to mire down in all this horror had just been added to the thread. It was too late.

18 weeks ATA: I asked my brother today what it was like for him, being involved in that desperate situation. Ironically, he dealt with the attack itself fairly well, so I guess I didn't give him enough credit. Immediately upon receiving the information about where I was and what was happening, his brain triggered an automatic protective mode, leaving him in a state of nearly suspended animation. He likened it to floating in an aquarium tank, watching life happen through the glass, everything blurred through the water that surrounded him. At his periphery, he was vaguely aware of terrible thoughts, macabre images, like standing in an empty funeral home, looking at a flag draped across a coffin. Blood, so much blood, sprayed across some bathroom a world away in a hotel in Africa. But they couldn't reach him. They couldn't touch him as he sheltered in the deepest recesses of his own psyche, protected by his own mind. He didn't tell any of his friends what was happening. He didn't talk about it or cry. He simply shut off the majority of his cognitive function, kicking himself into some sort of autopilot that kept him walking around though he didn't have a destination in mind, and going to class even though he couldn't process what the professor was saying. He told me about trying to nap because holding himself in that suspended state was exhausting him, although he didn't realize why he was so tired at the time. But he couldn't sleep. He just lay there, staring at the ceiling or the back of his eyelids, living in that space insomniacs so often occupy, in between being awake and asleep. And his brain mercifully kept him from thinking anything, though the anxiety right there at the edge of the tank was tapping on the glass, trying to get his attention, keeping him from sleeping. That's the thing about the protective aquarium – and believe me I've felt like that, with ten feet of water between me and my loved ones and friends, their words coming to me across an abyss, slurred and hard to decipher – is that in order to protect you, it temporarily muffles everything around you, but eventually those terrible thoughts tapping on the glass catch up with you. So hours and hours later, when Max got the news that I was out, it wasn't relief that he felt. It was the sensation of the aquarium shattering all around him in a single instant, spilling him back into the real world, which was entirely too close and overwhelming. It was the sensation of trying to answer all the hard, dark questions his brain had not let him ask himself about humanity for the past day. It was the sensation of trying to gasp for breath, when he hadn't even realized that for over a dozen hours, he had been holding his. So instead of allowing himself to be tortured for so many hours of uncertainty, he experienced the full trauma all at once when the glass broke, like a swift right hook to the jaw, leaving him feeling the entire spectrum of emotions, mixed with a desperate sort of nausea and desire to throw up, just from the sheer impact of it all.

Part Four:
The Good Guys

My phone rang. My hotel room phone. Or, technically, both of them. The one next to the bed, and the one everyone forgets about: the one mounted next to the toilet. It scared the metaphorical shit out of me. My breath caught instantly, and I froze. Why in the FUCK would my hotel room phone be ringing? Who knew I was here? Would the terrorists really call me? And if nothing else, I desperately wanted the phone to shut the hell up; it was the loudest noise inside my actual bathroom since the fire alarm had started going off. My instinct to minimize noise was screaming to turn the phone off, but I didn't know how to make it stop other than to answer it, and I certainly was not about to do that. I told the security team my phone was ringing, and they were baffled. I hung up with them and called Marine Post One back, but the gruff man who answered was equally bemused. Just as I was about to hang up with him, though, he told me to hold on. He covered the mouthpiece, so I could only hear the muffled sound of voices; it seemed like he had asked some sort of question and then another, deeper voice had responded. He asked if I was still there and I said that yes of course I was. He told me that if my phone rang again, I should answer it. Then, just as he said that, like a perfect scene in a movie, my phone rang again. I stared at it. I took a deep breath and told MPO to stay on the phone with me because I was going to answer it. Then, shaking, I took the receiver off the wall, and in a tiny, whispered voice, said, "Hello?"

Working out was the first salvation I found. It was incredibly hard to go to gyms at first. Gyms are a hotspot for loud and unexpected noises. I would be in a panic the first 30-40 minutes inside a gym. I would make Paul or mom come with me. I would hyper focus on the lack of exits. I would scrutinize people's faces and bags as they walked in, wondering if they were there to work out or to commit a mass shooting. I would spend the majority of my time thinking about how to escape or hide in the case of the latter. I certainly couldn't wear headphones or focus on a workout. But slowly it started to feel normal again. Slowly it started to feel safe again. It gave me something I wasn't scared of. A place to leave my apartment and go. It gave me something I was in control of. It gave me progress when I felt like everything else in my life was regressing. I work out now, maniacally, and it reminds me of my old self. It gives me a sense of pride and something to care about on the days I don't care about anything. It gives me some hope. A reason to love myself and be kind to myself when otherwise I have none. And to Paul who picked me up off the floor crying more than once and convinced me to go to the gym through my tears and panic and screaming that I couldn't do it, thank you. I know that isn't enough, but thank you.

A dead-calm male voice responded to me, in an American accent. He knew my name, and he was asking me how I was holding up. I was so stunned that it was hard for me to respond. I whispered some sort of sound that was like an assent and he went on with an explanation that sounded prepared and businesslike. He told me they had set up a security outpost at the reception desk in the lobby, and that if I needed anything I could now call down. I was at a complete loss for words. The gunshots were still going on above me. I knew the hostages were still fighting for their lives. What the hell did he mean, security outpost? What the hell did he mean I could call down if I needed anything? I needed a lot of things! First and foremost, I needed to get the fuck out of the hotel! But I couldn't come up with a response; I was worried I was having some sort of hallucination. All I got out was, "What?!" He was still calm, his voice patient and reassuring in its businesslike manner. He was speaking as if there was absolutely nothing out of the ordinary about the situation, about the call, about a security outpost. Finally, it dawned on me: they must have set up a way to forward calls from reception to some safe room they had at another property nearby. He must be some sort of Marine Post One extension. Although, if that was the case, why hadn't MPO known who was calling? I had been awake for over twenty hours, every nerve was completely frayed, and I had no ability to make sense of what he was saying. But then again, I really hadn't been able to make sense of my reality at all for the last twelve hours so what did it matter? I asked him if he was really at reception, like literally in the hotel lobby. It was the only thing I could think to say. He couldn't understand me though, because of my terrified, shaky whisper, so he told me that whispering was unnecessary now as my floor had been secured. My jaw dropped. Was this guy kidding? Was he even real? Had I finally lost my fucking mind? What the hell did that even mean? Why could I still hear gunshots then?! "Uhhh... I am going to keep whispering," was all I could manage. He said that was fine. I repeated my question about his location, and he confirmed that yes indeed, they were literally at the reception desk. The desk where I had checked in just days prior. The desk I had passed on my way to my room thirteen hours ago, before this nightmare had started. They, and I had no clue who the hell 'they' even were, other than really calm American guys, were here, just downstairs.

4 weeks ATA: I am on a bender of watching documentaries about extraordinary humans. My all-time favorite story for over a decade has been that of the rugby team that crashed in the Andes Mountains in the '70s and had to resort to cannibalism to survive, ultimately having two of their members hike out, without gear and half-starved, to save the remaining survivors. It is not the morbid details of the cannibalism or how they lived on the mountain that has caused me to retell this story a million times to friends and colleagues alike. It is the extraordinary resilience of those men. It is their inability, or perhaps unwillingness, to give up. And the fact that, when they did finally make it out, they had a newfound appreciation for the things that really matter in life: passion, love and joy. And they built new lives centered around those things. I have thought of those men so many times since getting back from the terrorist attack. I have thought of them and berated myself for my inability to turn my life upside down and recenter it around what really matters. Instead I feel sluggish, irritable, miserable. I hardly find the will to live at all some days, and at times physically cannot pick myself up off the ground. I lie there and sob and think that I wish I was more like Nando, the man who led the hike out of those mountains, but that I just am not. I don't have whatever he has. There is no point in me being alive, I have absolutely no ability to overcome adversity. But minutes or hours later, when the tears stop and I have exhausted every emotion I have, I watch another documentary about another amazing human. Because even if I am not in their class, not even close, it gives me hope to know that humans like that exist. It makes me want to live, if only to see their feats. So thank you to Jimmy Chin for coming back to your true passion and your inspiring career after the terrifying avalanche that almost took your life. Thank you, Conrad, for leading the expedition to Meru, and being absolutely unwilling to give up until you reached the summit. Thank you, especially, to Renan who healed like Superman from a near-fatal ski accident, only to then have to overcome a stroke in order to reach an impossible goal. I think of you and your superhero-like feats often. Thank you to Alex Honnold in Free Solo, for knowing when to push forward and break records, but also for knowing when not to. That takes as much courage as it does smarts. Thank you to Tommy Caldwell, a truly phenomenal human, for overcoming a trauma like mine and channeling that, heartbreak and a lost finger into becoming one of the greatest climbers of all time. And finally, a big thanks to KJ in the Dawn Wall, for flat out refusing to give up, even when you started to lose faith in yourself. I watched you try that pitch over and over, day after day, and thought that I would have given up a million times. So now when I want to quit, I think of you, and how ultimately, through sheer persistence and determination, you made it. Thank you all for showing us that the greatest hurdles in life are not the walls we climb physically, but the obstacles we face in our minds. You all are truly inspirations to me.

My shock must have been palpable, and his voice became urgent for a moment as he explained that even though he was just downstairs, and my floor was secure, it was absolutely imperative that I stay in my room a while longer. The entire building was, obviously, not yet safe, so my room was the safest place for me to be. It was all so bizarre. The world had once again been turned on its head. I had no idea what to say. It occurred to me that I had no idea who the hell he even was, so I asked him. He said he was my security liaison. In the upside down and backward world I was living in, I didn't even think to ask a follow up question. I just said ok. He said he would be in touch again shortly with updates, and that sounded great, so I said ok again. It seemed like he was about to hang up, so, desperate for comfort, I asked him if he was absolutely sure my floor was secure, whatever that even meant. He confirmed it was. I hung up, genuinely stunned. I stared at the receiver for a moment, trying to process that phone call as well as the shots that were still going off upstairs. I was slightly comforted, but at least equally confused. I texted my family a quick description of the call and played back a quick summary of it for MPO as well, who no longer seemed at all surprised. I hung up with MPO and called the security team back. My family responded asking me what the hell a 'security liaison' is, but I had no answer for them. I was completely at a loss for anything that made an iota of sense. But all I could picture was this American guy, this calm American guy, shuffling papers at the front desk and getting things organized. In my mind he was a lanky white guy, with brown eyes, and he was dressed kind of like a 1920s detective. It was nice to have something, anything, else to think about other than the explosions happening just two floors away. As I envisioned this security liaison in the lobby, I could hear another phone ringing in another room. It rang and rang, and I figured the person in that room was too afraid to answer, as I had been. I wished desperately that I could tell whoever that was that it was ok to answer, that they would feel much better if they did. It was our security liaison with some updates! And suddenly I felt warmer and safer than I had in so many hours, thinking that he was calling around comforting people. I hugged my knees up to my chest, leaned my forehead against them, and started repeating to myself, 'My floor is secure, my floor is secure, my floor is secure,' just waiting for my next phone call.

7 weeks ATA: I can read again!!!! Oh thank goodness. I still can't read for very long, but I sat down by the fire and read a few chapters of a book today. It was like heaven. I could focus on the words, they didn't blur together, and I understood the concepts and the plot. For an hour, I felt like a normal human being. For an hour, I felt like myself. A baby step, maybe, but today it feels like I leapt across the moon. Oh thank goodness for baby steps.

I started hearing these thuds above me. It's hard to explain, but even in all the ruckus, they stood out because, despite being rather muffled, I could hear that they were incredibly rhythmic. By that time, I was quite certain that it wasn't the sound of gunfire, as I was very accustomed to that particular sound, and its unpredictable pacing, which was always far from rhythmic. This new thudding was paced, and it was coming through my bathroom ceiling. There would be a few thuds, then a long silence, then more paced thudding. It was loud, but not like explosives. I wondered at first if it was boots all marching at a very particular pace, with regular pauses, but my brain told me that was not quite right. The thuds endured for the next few hours, and I never could figure out what they were, but it was an amusing puzzle for my brain to spin on at times. I even fumbled with the bathroom receiver for a minute, trying to call my security liaison back and ask him, figuring he must know as he seemed pretty with it. But I realized that I didn't have the shortcut buttons on the bathroom receiver that I was used to on a hotel phone, so I wasn't exactly sure how to call reception. I dialed zero, but that didn't work. So I just sat there, puzzled, listening to the thudding and hoping that it was a good sound, an American sound, that somehow signaled the impending end of the terrorists.

There is a little group inside the FBI whose sole job is to deal with trauma victims. They even have special paperwork for American citizens who were victims of terrorist attacks abroad. Isn't that just wildly specific? I am so incredibly thankful for these folks. These are the people who were waiting for me when I got off the plane in Ohio (or at least, they tried. I had made a slightly earlier flight out of Chicago than the one that was on my itinerary, so technically I evaded the

FBI, but it was an accident! They came to my parents' house a few hours later instead.) These are the folks who brought me a care package the first night I was back with a little stuffed elephant which I held while I cried later that week. These are the people who got my personal items back from the hotel in Kenya and delivered them to my house. Who reimbursed me for the flights I had to buy to get back from Africa in a hurry. And most importantly, these are the people who absolutely insisted I get a trauma therapist. In fact, they found me my trauma therapist, Dahlia, and told her to expect my call. They checked in with me repeatedly to make sure that I liked her and that I scheduled my first session. Then, that I had attended my first session and planned to go back. And when the FBI tells you to do something, you do it. In retrospect, I am even more grateful. So many people who have been through trauma are not forced to see a therapist, even though I wish they were. They don't have help to find a specialist, and they worry about the stigma and the costs and the time. But my therapist saved me, so many times and in so many different ways.

I asked Paul what he thought it meant *exactly* that this security liaison guy said my floor was secure. At first, it had been comforting, but after a while it was like I had wrung all the comfort out of the phrase and left myself these empty and meaningless words. The supposed security of my floor hadn't changed the sounds I was hearing. It hadn't changed the fact that I was still hiding on my bathroom floor. The same guy who had told me my floor was secure had also told me I absolutely had to stay where I was, and how did that make any sense anyway? Perhaps I had been clinging to this phrase that was ultimately hollow. But Paul was extremely comforting in his response. His tone was hard, calculating, and I loved that because I knew he was not trying to placate me, or tell me sweet nothings to calm me down. He was giving me his honest read, his honest analysis, of the phrase and the situation. He told me that his best guess was that there were good guys on my floor. On my floor! Like outside my door. Probably, there were good guys stationed on every floor other than five, ready to spring into action if the terrorists somehow tried to get away and move to another floor. They'd be ready to shoot anything that moves, which is why, he said, it was likely so important to stay in my room. I didn't want to go through over a dozen hours of this torture only to have my head blown off by the good guys because I had rushed out of my room in terror. That made sense. I pushed Paul again and again to basically repeat himself over text, because I loved the idea that there could be good guys right outside my door. Paul virtually guaranteed me at that point that the terrorists would never make it off the fifth floor alive. They would never make it to me. I cried. At least one threat was mostly eliminated. I would not be shot in the face by terrorists and left to bleed out on a bathroom floor. They would not break down my door and scream at me. I would not be taken, or tortured, or raped. I would not have to use the shards of glass on my floor to end my own life. If the whole goddamn building didn't collapse on my head, and no other bad guy forces showed up to aid the ones upstairs, I was going to live.

1 week ATA: Carolyn says there is something called Post Traumatic Growth. She says that at the end of a person's recovery journey, when they have processed the trauma in its entirety and have filed it away properly so that it doesn't run their life anymore, they often see the world with a new perspective. They often describe feeling like they have a new lease on life. In fact, she told me that they often ultimately feel thankful for their trauma. That's something I absolutely cannot fathom. This is the worst thing that has ever happened to me. I had this beautiful, wonderful life that made perfect sense and they took that away from me. I can't focus, I can't read, I can't sleep, I can't converse, I can't leave my house, I can't go to work. I can't do any of the things that used to bring me joy. I hate what happened to me in a deep way that is hard to put into words. I feel rage that I didn't even think I had the capacity to feel. My life is in tatters and it's all because of what happened in the hotel that day. I don't think I will end up feeling grateful. I would be happy if I could just forget this whole horrible thing ever happened and get my fucking life back.

The next call from my security liaison came a couple of hours later. Calm, again, and this time even more comforting and reassuring. He asked me if I was okay, and I said that yes, technically I was. He told me I was doing great. I don't know how one 'does great' waiting in a terrorist attack, but apparently just sitting there alone and terrified qualifies. He sounded like he knew what he was talking about. He asked me if I had food and water and I said yes. A couple of hours earlier, Paul had chastised me until I army crawled for a granola bar and a sparkling water out of the mini bar. Paul had said it was imperative I stay nourished as it would help me stay alert, but after dragging the food and water back to the bathroom, I had barely been able to keep any down. A few sips of water and a single bite of the granola bar were all I could consume before I felt like another tiny bit in my stomach would certainly cause me to throw up. And that would be loud, and thereby unsafe. So I just placed them in the corner of the bathroom, figuring if my hunger or thirst magically returned, they'd still be there. After telling my security liaison that yes, I had food, I wanted some answers. First, I asked him if they were evacuating the hotel and he said no, sounding rather surprised. He said that no one was coming in or out, and that I would need to stay put as it was the safest thing for me at the moment. That moment was really important, because that was when I decided to trust him. He didn't give me false hope, he didn't say people were coming when they weren't, and not only did he seem confident, he was sitting in the goddamn lobby so he would fucking know. And for the rest of the time, he was the one and only person who always provided me with correct information. It was a great comfort. I was also bound and determined to get a more legitimate answer for myself and my family about who in the heck he was. This time I specified, and instead of asking him who he was, I asked him who he was *with*. But he sort of coughed and snuffled into the phone as if that was an answer. I almost laughed, every single word had been perfectly intelligible up to that point, but this I couldn't understand? No way. I asked him to repeat that. After hesitating for a moment, he replied, "Uhh, ma'am, I'm with the Embassy." Now that sounded legitimate. I thanked him, asked him if my floor was still secure, which he affirmed, and hung up the phone. But I couldn't get over the idea of it. The Embassy! So usually this guy sits at a desk filling out paperwork, and today he is sitting at the front desk of a hotel that is actively under attack? This guy must have drawn the short straw at work today!

Tuesdays ATA: On Tuesdays I see my therapist. It's funny, it's become respected and revered, almost a religious day in my little family. My parents purposely don't ask me any logistics questions on Tuesday, but they often call to check in. Paul knows I will be introverted and glass eyed. My friends know I will be slow to respond, quiet, withdrawn. But I think what none of them knows is that on Tuesdays I feel the best. On Tuesdays, I pour everything out in therapy, and for the rest of the day, I am empty. Empty in a way that doesn't feel sad or depressing, but in a way that feels comforting. There is nothing boiling and bubbling just below the surface. I don't need to keep myself distracted with a million to-do list items so that a thousand emotions don't come spilling forth and totally overwhelm my loved ones. On Tuesdays, I am exhausted, but I am not broken. On Tuesdays, I have hope.

I texted this to the group text with my parents, Paul and my brother. They were also thrown off that this guy was from the Embassy, but ultimately it made sense to all of us. We knew they were involved, certainly. And no matter where this guy was from, he was giving us all a sense of hope, and of calm. Until we got a text from Peter, from Kenyan Special Forces. He said once again that the evacuation team was on the way to get me. Interestingly, I didn't feel thankful or excited that time, but I didn't feel skeptical either. I felt worried. The American guys were calm. The American guys had told me that it would be American forces that would come get me and take me out of the hotel. I had started having grand fantasies about being flown back to the US on Airforce One. I wanted those guys, the best in the world. I had become very attached to the idea. Not the guys who had said a million times before that they were coming to get me but had yet to show up. And the Americans had also told me that they wanted to eliminate the terrorists before saving me, which still sounded like a pretty good idea to me, and as I listened to the gunshots above me, I started to panic. Why would KSF come get me now?! The terrorists were clearly still alive! And I didn't want to go with them, I wasn't supposed to go with them! How would they even hand me off to the American forces!? What if I got sort of lost in the shuffle, or worse, what if I was killed in the extraction attempt?! But it was then that we got an update that implied that the last couple of living terrorists had suicide vests themselves. That information was accompanied by the following words: "If KSF comes to get you, go with them." The fear of the building collapsing on me was back. The hope had been extinguished once again.

I have developed a tic. It's a coping mechanism, I think. When sordid details come up about the attack, or someone asks me an incredibly insensitive question, or I am trying to do something normal but a flashback clouds my vision, I clear my throat. Quietly, once or twice. I clear my throat and it's like I am also clearing my thoughts. I try to empty my consciousness of anything related to the attack and replace it with something else, anything else. I give myself a second to gather my thoughts and my words, and instead of giving into instinct which tells me to scream or run, I can then respond calmly or continue the task I am working on. It's the only way to stay somewhat sane and look like a normal, unimpeded person.

We were all starting to get frustrated with the rampant misinformation, especially when it seemed purposeful. Not all of it was that way, of course – Kenyan Special Forces obviously told me a few times they were on their way without actually being able to come get me, but I understood and appreciated that they had far bigger problems they were dealing with, and the nature of their problems was inherently unpredictable. They were doing their best and putting their lives on the line to do so, and I am endlessly thankful for that. The changes in updates couldn't be helped, that even happened with Marine Post One. But some of the misinformation seemed more premeditated. I was told a couple of hours into the attack that Kenya's President had tweeted that the hotel had been secured. That was so incredibly false it barely deserved a response given that we were still cowering in our rooms at that point, listening to the gunshots and explosions; it only made sense to me if he had been trying to paint a picture of a country far safer for tourists than the one he was actually running. Why else tweet such blatantly false information when your Special Forces are on site actively attempting to quell the attack? Why else cause my family, and so many other victims' families, to sigh with relief that their loved ones were finally safe, when we weren't even close? Why else cause such confusion in the news that the reports *still are not correct to this day*? It was truly infuriating, and while purposeful misinformation is always frustrating, this was literally life or death. My life or death. And so this was not just frustrating but infuriatingly reckless. It scarred my family and increased the whiplash and oscillation of the furious roller coaster they endured for seventeen hours. It gave new, deeply painful meaning to the term 'alternative facts.'

8 weeks ATA: Today I checked an email account I don't use often. I had an email from a strange address I didn't recognize. When I opened it, I slowly realized it was a bill. A bill from the DusitD2 Hotel in Nairobi. A bill from the place where I came so close to losing my life. The hotel had sent me a bill for my meals and amenities while I was staying there. Including but not limited to breakfast the day of the fucking attack. That fucking hotel wanted their $40 so badly, that they charged my credit card. They sent me an email with my folio and a line that said (typo and all), "We thank you for your support during these difficult moments the hotel has gone through." I was seeing fucking red. My hands were shaking, and I had tears of rage in my eyes. The hotel whose security forces had failed us. The hotel where I almost died wanted their fucking money for the meals that nearly ended my life. Did they send these to everyone?! Did these fucking folios go to the families of the innocent people who lost their lives in the attack that day?! How. Fucking. Dare. They. I started yelling to Paul, and I was completely inconsolable. I thought he would take my side, but he was calm, he didn't seem to think it mattered at all. He kept trying to tell me that in the scheme of things it was unimportant, to put it aside. My rage spiraled; it was all-consuming. I screamed at him that these people are assholes, I screamed at him to agree with me, these fucking people, how dare they. I screamed at him and he looked at me sadly, with pity and concern, which made me scream more, that I wasn't being unreasonable or *out of control, but that this was absolutely unconscionable and I didn't see why the hell he wouldn't just agree with me. I was truly out of control. He finally said, still dead calm, that it's true, it was unreasonable and thoughtless. But that at the end of the day, the hotel is a business. They don't care about people, they just care about money, and we shouldn't be surprised. I couldn't talk to him for hours; I was so furious. Why couldn't he just support me? Didn't he understand everything that I had been through? It took that long for me to calm down. It took that long for me to start sobbing. All I wanted when I was on the floor of that bathroom was to get home to Paul. Now here I was, screaming at him. What the hell was wrong with me? I cried and cried and cried, just lying face down on the carpet in our living room. I couldn't get up. I kept telling him I was so sorry, and then for a long time I was just silent. He tried to comfort me; he tried to hold me, but I couldn't bear to be touched – I didn't deserve to be comforted. I felt like a monster. Maybe I am one.*

After we were in the double-digit hours, my parents started trying to make jokes. I appreciated it but couldn't actually laugh. It was clear that they were trying to signal their belief that I would be ok. But the jokes were as forced as my almost-laughter. I would just respond: "Ha." But it was comforting in a strange way. If they had been sharing their favorite childhood memories or telling me how much they were going to miss me, it certainly would have added to my terror. But the more they joked, the surer they must have been that I was going to live, which helped me be more confident that I was going to live. They also told me to have the security team book me a flight straight back to Ohio for as soon as I could get out, and they started talking about the things we would do together. They talked about going shopping, and hugging me, and watching movies in front of the fireplace. My mom said I should even accompany her to an appointment with her doctor because she wouldn't want to be away from me for a single instant. Those things were comforting, too. It made me believe in this sliver of hope, this unlikely but possible future in which I lived through the attack and saw my family again. It made the smallest portion of my brain put hope in that possibility. I pushed it away consciously, not wanting to again cling to hope that might never come. But in the back of my head, in the deepest recesses of my soul, that hope grew into a little seedling, and it comforted me greatly. Death was no longer a certainty, and it was my parents' change in behavior that truly signaled it, that made me want to believe it.

18 weeks ATA: I asked my mom what the whole experience has been like for her, because she never talks about it. What's extraordinary is that in my time in that hotel, we were so much more connected than I even knew. She described the exact same initial physical response, her heart hurting so badly it felt like it might explode. She told me, without ever having heard me express it, that when I went silent for a little while, she found herself hoping desperately that if the terrorists had gotten to my room, I had found a way to kill myself. She said she had been wild with the thought that I could not go with them, could not let myself end up being tortured and raped. It was dark, but I smiled a small smile when she told me that, thinking that even my most private thought had been shared with her that day, so in a way I really had never been as alone as I'd felt.

But she also told me that in many ways the hardest part has been trying to connect with me since I've been home. We are very close, or at least we were, often talking on the phone every other day. But she said in these weeks and months following the attack, she has become afraid to talk to me, afraid to call. My moods are so erratic, and she feels like everything she says makes me upset, and she worries that she is retarding my ability to heal. She said she calls her own mom instead, crying and explaining to her how she doesn't know how I am doing because she is afraid to call me. It made me so sad to picture that, and see her tears start to roll as she talked about it. My mom is really tough, probably the toughest person I know. For her to give way to tears means she is really hurting, really at a loss. I tried to explain to her that she can't make me worse, just like she can't make me better. That I just have good days and bad days, and when she catches me on a bad day there's nothing she can do. I tried to tell her that when I scream at her, it isn't personal. The battle is not with her but with my own brain, my own psyche. I explained how I told Paul not to take it personally and that she should do the same. But I know it must be really hard. I know how shitty I feel after I scream at her for no reason. I can't even imagine what it's like to be on the receiving end of that when all you want is to help your kid. When all you want is for her to be better, but what you see is a human in tatters, whom you can't fix, and you can't reach. It must be a truly terrible thing.

My phone rang again, the third call from the outpost in the lobby. I picked up incredibly quickly that time. The voice was as calm as always, and even more comforting because it was becoming familiar. It was, quite literally, my lifeline. This time the update was a bit different though; he wasn't just checking in. He wanted to update me on the operational plan. He told me that the good guys were going to begin the "final assault" very soon. He told me it was going to be very loud and very long, but not to lose heart because I should remember that every sound I was going to hear was a good thing. He told me to remember that with every sound, the good guys were finishing off the terrorists and getting closer to saving me. He told me that when it was over, he would try to call me back before they came to my room to get me, but more importantly, that whether or not he was able to call ahead of time, they would come get me when it was over. The American guys. They would come save me when the 'threat' had been 'eliminated' once and for all. He cautioned me, however, that it could take a very, very long time. He told me that I should settle in, and I wanted to laugh, because what the fuck had I been doing for the last sixteen hours? But he had been kind and correct in all his updates, so I just said, 'Ok,' in a tiny little voice, as my brain struggled under the realization that even after sixteen hours of absolute misery and terror, this could still be so far from over. No part of me knew, no part of me had even the slightest inkling, that whenever the attack finally ended, whether it was in minutes or hours or days, it would still be so very far from over.

14 weeks ATA: My therapist says I will be starting Prolonged Exposure (PE) treatment. It's like a sick joke. She says I will sit on her couch and, with my eyes closed, describe the worst parts of the terrorist attack to her, over and over, in

*the present tense as if it is once again happening to me. She
wants me to imagine the scene all around me, describing
what I am thinking and feeling and smelling and seeing, so
that it feels like it is really happening all over. Like I am back
in that bathroom. I want to scream: "Don't you think the attack itself was prolonged enough fucking exposure?!" But I
don't say anything. I just nod. She says that while I tell these
memories, I will record myself, so that every day between
therapy sessions I can play it back and listen. She says I
should do the same things then, closing my eyes and trying
to picture the scene perfectly, as if it's happening again. In
addition, I get to make a list of the things and places that
now scare me most, so when I am not listening to my recordings, my other homework is that I have to go spend time in
places I hate, like hotels and crowded restaurants. She says I
have to prove to myself that these things are not dangerous,
even though spending time in them will be miserable. What a
fucking blast. This is what trauma recovery looks like. It's
ugly and horrible and painful. PE has the highest rate of
people quitting of any PTSD treatment, and it is no wonder
why. You go through the worst experience of your life, make
it out alive, and your new job is to relive it over and over and
over until, supposedly, it hurts less. Oh, the fucking irony.*

It took a few minutes for the final assault to begin. It
felt like every muscle, every nerve, every sense was
straining in anticipation. My back was in considerable
pain, my arms and legs were so tight. My ears were ringing in the lull, knowing it was temporary, as they listened
to find out if this next bout of noise would kill or save me.
My brain was racing. I realized that it had been almost
thirty hours since I had gotten any rest at all. Without any

conscious thought or effort on my part, I had pulled an all-nighter, a feat I had found difficult even as a college student. Coherent thoughts were becoming hard to form in any manner. I recognized, after a moment, that I needed to update my family, so I told them, verbatim, what my security liaison had said. I had no energy left to feel anything, so I didn't try to spin it or give any opinion at all about this final assault. They pretended to be happy, but I could tell they were worried. Paul cautioned me to stay calm and stay put, saying that he wouldn't be surprised if it really did take several more hours, if not another day. The thought of sitting in that room through another sunset, another dark, lonely night, made me want to scream. For a moment my sympathetic nervous system took over completely and told me to RUN before the shots started again. Before the final assault started, which could take so very long. It took my full concentration and what little rational thought I could muster to ignore the urge. My immense, heavy exhaustion actually helped because my body wanted to preserve the little bit of energy I had left unless it was absolutely necessary to expend it. I recognized a deep certainty that if left in that hotel too long, I would genuinely lose my mind. Especially if I continued to be unable to eat or to sleep. It was miserable. It was hell.

3.5 weeks ATA: Paul and I were trying to have date night last night, just dinner and a movie at home, and I was already a bit despondent (I have a lot of trouble these days making any decisions at all, no matter how insignificant, and the movie choice was driving me insane). Then I got distracted from the movie choice altogether thinking about the fact that maybe I really was going insane: all this past week I

107

kept telling myself that the attack didn't really happen to me, it couldn't have, that would be crazy, and shoving the memories away. I think it was a coping mechanism, but it made it feel like my brain was breaking, like I was slowly losing it. Sometimes, trauma recovery is that way. It makes you think you are going mad. You can't relate to your friends, you can't fit in. Your life is a weird, empty shell, that no longer fits you. It doesn't make sense to you. You don't care about what you used to care about, you don't care about what your friends care about. Your friends and family seem vapid, shallow, inconsiderate, naive. You don't understand how they can carry on about such idiotic things. The world is so dangerous, don't they know that? Your job seems pointless, your house seems pointless, your things seem pointless, working for money seems pointless, some days even living seems pointless. Your emotions swing like crazy, and the details of the memory haunt you, even as they fade and blur. Sometimes you realize something you thought you remembered wasn't even right. The order of the memory or some detail is off. How can you be wrong about the most terrifying day of your life? You must have lost it there. You must have lost your mind in the trauma. Because nothing makes sense, not your life and not your memories. Perhaps nothing is even real. Perhaps you have arrived at the only conclusion that matters and it's that nothing matters. Or perhaps you just need one single good goddamn night of sleep!

The final assault was indeed quite long and loud. I wouldn't have thought it was possible to adjust to the cacophony, to the fear, but after sixteen hours in that misery, I did start to. I would still jump each time the shooting and grenades and artillery started back up, but it was a small jump. It was not a jump of surprise. I had internalized that there would always be more shooting, always. That I might just die there, eventually, of hunger or thirst while the shooting raged on and on, forever. I was losing my ability to track the sounds or try to identify them or figure out which direction they were coming from, but I was also losing my ability to track my emotions, or stir up any feelings of hope whatsoever. It was like a tiny bundle of tinder, blowing in the wind. A small flame of hope would kick up in the lulls of sound, only to be blown out by the next bout of shooting. And eventually, I no longer wanted to fan the flame. I was too tired, physically, mentally and emotionally. If the building collapsed and killed me, so be it. If they still figured out a way to come shoot me, so be it. It felt true that I would never leave the hotel, but I had lost the ability to care. I leaned back on a towel I had balled up and closed my eyes. Even as the shooting raged on, I started drifting in and out of consciousness, the exhaustion besting the fear for about thirty seconds at a time. I would slam back into a sitting position upon waking, listening to the sounds, trying to see if they had gotten closer, or if I could tell if the good guys were gaining an advantage, if this might ever end. But then the hope would die again, the exhaustion would take over, and I would drift back into a terrified, dreamless sleep for another thirty seconds. In total, I got maybe five full minutes of sleep that way. I felt that hope die so many times that I would be surprised if I can ever feel hope again, the way that I used to. I started actively suppressing it, even the whispers of hope were wearing me out, and I had nothing left to give. I had no hope left, only a thin strand remained of a now distant will to live. A memory of how badly I wanted to get out, which I clung to with the tiny bit of mental strength I had left, while I drifted in and out.

2 weeks ATA: I guess I'm still too angry to think about solutions. I don't really believe it yet. I don't believe there is a fix. Even humans working toward the betterment of mankind would fight and war over the best path forward. What do you do? How do you get people to change? To change their beliefs. Is it dialogue? Forced empathy? Learning that humans (and thereby the self) are malleable and that that's inherently awesome? Is it by somehow involving their own self-interest? Is it about pride? Money? Success? Love? Freedom? What do you do.

Every few minutes my dad would text and ask if I could still hear shooting. Sometimes I would say that at the moment all was quiet, but then, inevitably, the shooting would start again. We were all, except for Paul, baffled and frustrated with how long it was going on. I think the frustration, exhaustion, worry and impotence all combined to finally break my dad's spirit about sixteen and a half hours in. He must have thought that the longer the final assault raged on, the less likely I was to make it out. He must have thought, as I had so many hours before, that it was time to say goodbye. His tone changed completely from seeking information, to a soft, light, loving tone that I know well, but which was choked with emotion. He texted me asking if I remembered when, as a small child, he would pretend to smell my feet and exaggeratedly tell me how stinky they were. I loved this game, so I would immediately start laughing, and say, "No daddy, they smell like roses!" Which somehow was the signal for him to start tickling my feet, at which point I would just laugh and laugh and laugh. He reiterated that memory over text and then told me how much he loved me. It was more than I could take. I couldn't respond. The texts terrified me to the core. I recognized, even in that instant, that sharing childhood memories, which he hadn't done for the endless, terrifying hours that had preceded this, must mean he had come to the conclusion that I was suddenly in mortal danger. He had learned of something through the news or one of our contacts that I didn't know yet. It was the closest I came to breaking down the entire time. It was the only thing that tapped into an inner reserve of emotion that my survival instincts had put away. I recognized the danger of opening the flood gate and waited for someone to change the subject while I listened to the gunshots, trying to project my own plot onto the sound, about how the good guys were winning far faster than anyone anticipated, and that we were all going to live.

18 weeks ATA: My dad told me today that he and mom took turns during the attack, switching off who was texting me and who was breaking down. He said in retrospect it was pretty amazing that they never broke down at the same time, and they never yelled at each other. They had an urgency in their voices all day, but it was a shared urgency not irritation. Each time it was his turn, he had to force the negative thoughts away actively, and he would just say to himself over and over that it was not if I got out but when. *That sometime in the near future, even though he couldn't picture it, he would get the call or text that told him I was safe. I asked him about that memory he had texted, wondering what had made him share it, and he shrugged. He hesitated and then said, "I never would've forgiven myself if I hadn't." I realized for the first time that I had read it all wrong. He had been trying to distract me with a happy childhood memory. He had been trying to give me something nice to think about instead of all the horror that was surrounding me in the hotel. He was not in possession of new and damning information. He was just trying, from halfway around the world, to comfort his terrified daughter.*

When I had finally given up completely, when I had gotten used to the fact that the shooting would always start again, there was a knock on my door. Not a slamming, urgent sound. Not the sound of someone trying to rip the door off of its hinges, but just a regular knock. My heart leapt. I knew, as I had known instantly with the terrorists, who these men were. I knew they were the good guys. I jumped off the bathroom floor, leaving my backpack there, with my nibbled-on granola bar, my half-empty water bottle. Leaving this spot on the floor that had been my hideout for so many hours. And as I ran toward the bedroom, I could hear them. I could hear calm, American voices saying my name. They were asking if I was ok, saying that they were there to get me. I started sobbing instantly, and it made it hard to answer them. My voice was ruined, shaking, as I tried to process what was happening. It couldn't be true, right? It wasn't possible that I was really going to get to leave, after all that hell, all that terror. After telling my parents and Paul goodbye. After accepting and lamenting the loss of my life. But I decided that even if I was hallucinating, I needed to answer them. They were still saying my name, asking if I was inside, and for a moment I worried wildly that they might leave me.

That if I could not muster a sound, an answer, they would shrug and move on to save the next person and I would miss my chance. Through a gargled sob, I tried to ask them if I could un-barricade the door. I didn't want to start moving furniture if they were going to blow the door down, and I remembered Melissa's warning about the Kenyan Special Forces so many hours before. I held up the one hand I wasn't using to talk to the Google security team, to show that I was not a threat. They couldn't understand what I was saying though, through the thick door and all my sobs. So I just shook my head and shouted, "Can I open the door?!" They responded so calmly, reiterating that, yes, they were there to get me out, so if I could open the door that would be great.

Every single day ATA: When I got out alive, I thought it was over. But it's so far from over. Trauma recovery is the hardest thing I've ever done in my life.

By hour seventeen, I was on the phone with a guy named Cole from the security team. I don't know if he had been doing it for me, or for him, but he had been having me report what I was hearing and do my best to identify the direction the noises had come from, and then he would check it against his reports. His reports were always late, but I liked describing things to him because it made me feel like at least maybe, somehow, I was being helpful. Like maybe my reports could help save someone else. It had also been helping me to stay awake. So I was still on the phone with him and was still describing every sound I heard on autopilot, when they knocked on my door, which I immediately related to him. I was ecstatic, I couldn't wait to wrench the door open and run from the hotel, but Cole was skeptical. He kept urging me not to open my door until the men outside had officially identified themselves. I told Cole that their accents were distinctly American, but he said that was not enough. He asked me if I could see them through the peephole, so I looked out and the emotions finally overtook me completely. There were two American men standing there, calm as could be. They looked like nothing terrifying was happening, or ever had happened. They were in button-down shirts and khaki pants and bulletproof vests. I couldn't even see their guns. It was true, then, they were there to save me. And just as I had internalized the end of my life seventeen hours before, I started internalizing the fact that my life was not over after all. I could not answer Cole, I was so wracked with emotion, with sobs. He was still absolutely adamant that I get these men to identify themselves before I open the door, so as I was wrenching the furniture out of the way with strength I couldn't believe I had left, I shouted through the door, "Please, can you tell me who you're with?!" And just as I was reaching for the door handle to exuberantly throw it open and fall into their arms, the response made my hand freeze in place. The voice came clearly through the door, a bit of a snarl: "Don't worry about it."

2 weeks ATA: I didn't feel anything at first. I was in this immaculate state of shock that felt amazing. I got out of the attack and had only one thought really, and it was 'Holy shit, I lived.' I was so sure I was going to die, but then I didn't! I was going to see my family again, something I had truly believed I would never get to do. I was just so happy to get back to the United States. I was so happy to hold my loved ones. I talked with them and joked, told them stories in a lighthearted way, sat by the fire and smiled. But then, after being back for about two days, the depression crushed me like a freight train that I never even saw coming. Suddenly I was irritable. Suddenly I wasn't sure what the point of living through the attack was. Suddenly I was riddled with guilt and misery and torturous memories. I went from sleeping like a baby to being entirely unable to sleep. I went from jokes and smiles to an inability to converse. And the fact that I was upset instead of appreciating that I was alive made me absolutely hate myself, and spiral further. So many people died that day, what was the point of being alive if I didn't even appreciate it? I shouldn't have lived. There were other people in that hotel who had lost their lives who would have actually been able to appreciate making it out. I should be dead. I explained these feelings to Carolyn and told her that I felt so overwhelmed because when I first got out, I thought that was it, that I made it out so it was over. But now it didn't feel over at all. It felt like I was sitting on the ground, picking up these sharp broken pieces of who I used to be and desperately trying to fit them back together. But I kept cutting myself on the pieces, and the whole thing felt useless anyway because even if I did eventually fit the pieces back together, it would look like shit. Everyone would see the cracks and crevices. A broken mirror glued back together never looks like a beautiful new mirror again. There is no hiding the devastation that has been done to it. But what Carolyn said will stay with me for the rest of my life. She said why take the pieces and try to make them into the old mirror? Why not take them and make a mosaic? Make a piece of art that is even more beautiful than the boring old mirror.

Take the pieces and make something new and unique and incredible. Some days I believe I can do that, and some days I don't. But at least now I have a new goal. At least I have something to envision that keeps me from wishing I had just died that day in the hotel. I can take what happened to me and, even though I will never have my old life back the way it was, if I give it my absolute all, I can make something new and beautiful in a different way.

After the terrifying response of, 'Don't worry about it,' I could hear one of them smack the other and then say, "Sorry about that, Meyli. We are with the Embassy." I hesitated for only a moment. By that time I was so exhausted, and so confused, and so incredibly sick of being in that godforsaken hotel while it was blown to bits that I shrugged, told Cole it was fine, hung up, and started to open the door. Then I realized I should send my family a text to let them know I was getting out. I chose probably the worst words that I possibly could have, sending the group text a message that read, "They got me!!!"

6 weeks ATA: Something I have been thinking about a lot is what I want to change about my life now. How did I live it before, and where was my thinking incorrect? I am sure there are many answers to this question, but the one that strikes me is that BTA, my life was built around what's next. Paul used to try to remind me to 'enjoy the journey, too' but I hated that expression. It wasn't the 'journey' I enjoyed, but the culmination of the journey. The ultimate success of whatever I had been working for. And the ability to look back on it afterward and recognize that it was indeed successful. But that meant that I was always saying happiness and con-

tentedness were for the future. I was missing so many beauti-
ful moments in the present. I was prioritizing whatever
helped me get to the next rung of the imaginary ladder I was
climbing, without ever thinking about what I was missing out
on in order to do so. My job and my accomplishments were
the foundation of my entire identity, so embracing them and
adding to my list of accolades was the priority. But now,
looking back, I can see how sad and misplaced that was.
How much more I want to be than "Google Employee." I also
always used to joke that I was old, but having almost lost my
life far too soon I am now regularly astounded by all the
decades I still have the chance to live. These days I hope to
build my life around something else. I want to live in the now
but appreciate my longevity. I want to smell the roses while
appreciating that I will be doing so for many decades yet to
come. It is so beautiful to be young and in love and alive. I
don't want to miss a moment of that because I am waiting for
something else. I have everything I could ever want.

Opening that door was, and forever will be, the happiest moment of my life. Those men will be my heroes for as
long as I live, and that was not lost on me at the time.
They were standing there, calm and kind and strong,
reaching their arms out toward me, like angels at my door.
They were there to save me. The vision that I had tried to
imagine the last few hours, to push away the image of the
terrorists coming to kill me, was the one that had actually
come true, of these incredible, brave strangers winning
the day and saving my life. I was awestruck. It was absolutely incredible – it still is – that in the situation that I
would have done absolutely anything to get out of, they
walked in voluntarily to save the lives of total strangers.

They didn't have to come help me. They didn't have to save my life. They didn't have to be brave and strong and heroic and amazing. They didn't have to be halfway around the planet, away from their families, risking their lives for people they had never met. But they were. And the ecstasy I felt at that moment does not have words that can describe it. I collapsed toward them, sobbing, "Thank you," over and over and over.

The human condition is inherently defined by the spectrum of good and evil. What's truly extraordinary is that that day I stood, physically, in between the extremes. Above me, men I didn't know held hostages and threatened their lives after having killed and ravaged innocent and unarmed civilians. They would kill me too, instantly and without regret, if given half a second to do so. On my floor and below me were strangers, total strangers to me, who had rushed into this nightmare to save my life, save all of our lives. The most terrifying experience I could ever have imagined, and they'd entered voluntarily. Men and women like that are what keep this whole world from going to shit. I cannot put into words the gratitude I feel for all the soldiers, British, American and Kenyan, who worked together to save us that day. And I will never forget for as long as I live that the human condition is a spectrum and every single one of us has to choose – very carefully and very consciously – where we are going to fall on that spectrum.

The two men, these two amazing strangers, were calm and businesslike, just as the voice on the phone had been, which was reassuring. It made me inhale deeply on instinct, to hold my sobs back, and focus on their words.

They first asked me if I had a bag. I was so happy to be able to say yes, it was like I had prepared properly, like I had the right answer. I said I had a small backpack and they smiled like they were proud of my forethought, which of course had actually been Melissa's. I described the bag and where it could be found in the bathroom, and one of them went to grab it for me while the other waited with me at the door. Then they asked me if I could walk, which I thought was such a bizarre question. I had the overwhelming urge to respond, "Walk?! I want to SPRINT out of this hellhole!" Instead I just said shakily, "Yes, I think so." They nodded politely and I stepped out into the hallway with them. Out of the hotel room. Out of that place where I had hidden for seventeen hours, fearing for my life and waiting for the moment when I would die, when my family would realize it had been too long since the last text, and that there wouldn't be another. Out of that nightmare. Out of the worst day, and night, of my life. Out, out, out. It was sublime.

4 weeks ATA: I have reversed my lifelong stance that I would never allow guns in my house. I used to fear them, used to worry that if we had one in the house, it would inevitably end up being part of some tragic accident, a child's life lost in the process. Guns were this over-the-top, completely unnecessary possession, which could be replaced with baseball bats if the motive for owning them was really self-defense. Suddenly, however, that phrase that I had always heard and dismissed as trite held real meaning: "The bad guys will have guns. You have to be able to protect yourself." The bad guys did in fact have guns; I had seen them. I had wanted nothing more than a weapon for those seventeen hours on that bathroom floor. A gun in my hand would have changed the entire experience. It would have given me back some power. Would have given me some hope. So instead of continuing to fear firearms, I learned everything I could about handling guns: how to aim by looking down the sights, how to breathe as you pull the trigger to ensure your shot goes off nice and straight, how to take a gun apart, how to clean it, how to check, very quickly, to see whether or not there is a bullet in the chamber, etc. I wanted to feel like if a bad guy even thought about coming in, Paul and I were protected, given that we were both comfortable with and knowledgeable about firearms. I see now that was all there ever was to it: guns are not something to avoid out of fear. They are something to understand, to appreciate the innate danger of, to respect, to keep locked away, very safely, unless and until they are absolutely necessary. And in the unlikely case of a truly dangerous situation in my home, I certainly wanted one on my side. Gun ownership isn't something I ever thought I would be so comfortable with, but it also feels right, because now I can sleep just a little better at night.

There was broken glass everywhere, absolutely everywhere. There was so much underfoot in the hallway and on the stairs that I was sliding, and my two escorts had to catch me and help hold me up more than once. Dimly, I was thankful for Melissa once again as I registered how terrible it would have been to be in sandals trying to make it through this cutting quicksand. I registered as we made it down the hallway that, just as I had concluded so many hours before, the giant window that backed the stairwell had indeed been blown inward. That was the cause of so much of the glass I was slipping on. The shock was intense, especially as it combined with my exhaustion and lack of food or sleep. I wasn't really processing that I was going to live. I wasn't really processing anything except what was directly in front of me. Then, with effort, I tried to remember what advice Melissa had given me about leaving the property so many hours before. It came back to me in wisps that she had said to look only at my feet. I did so, which helped me focus on not falling down because of all the slip-sliding glass. Then as I felt their arms under mine, supporting me, I realized I desperately wanted to know one thing which occurred to me all of a sudden. I asked if either of them had been the man on the phone. One of the men nodded at the other and said, "Yep, that was Carter." So his name was Carter. I had barely even realized that the man I had put more faith in than god the last few hours had been nameless in my head. He was 'my security liaison' or 'the guy from the Embassy.' But he was neither of those things. He was Carter, and I repeated his name in my head, as I still do sometimes, as they half-led, half-carried me down the stairs.

5 weeks ATA: My brother called me today, wracked with sobs. I couldn't understand him at first, but soon he was able to articulate what had happened: he had broken up with his girlfriend. It was his first serious girlfriend and he simply could not understand how he could love someone but not want to be with them. He worried that it truly meant he was a bad person. And he was absolutely mortified at the thought of having hurt someone he really cared about. I froze to the spot, and just stood there, listening to him, trying to soothe him and tell him that he's not a bad person.

That a bad person wouldn't care about hurting someone else. A bad person wouldn't be honest and tell the person they care about that they just don't see a future. I tried to tell him he had done the right thing. And I smiled a little to myself for two reasons: one, that at age 18 we really think that our first serious relationship that ends in a breakup is the end of the world. There was so much perspective for him to gain and so much to learn, and this was an important step. But ultimately, he would look back and laugh one day and say, 'Wow, yes I was so torn up over that. How naive we are at 18!' And two, because I was doing it. I was comforting someone else. I was his shoulder to cry on, and he had called me and allowed me to help. For that instant, I had a piece of myself back. It was proof absolutely positive that I could get there again. I could make room to put my family and friends first again. I could, if only for a short while, put the goddamn terrorist attack away, and comfort someone else.

As we neared the bottom of the staircase, Carter and his amazing friend, I will call him Sam because I don't know his name, started yelling. I almost passed out from fear. They screamed, "Blue, blue, blue!" Before I could move or run or scream, this password was returned from many male voices downstairs. I exhaled a sigh of deep relief, realizing it was some sort of code to let the people below know that we were good guys. Perhaps that was the first time it registered in the back of my head that bad guys must still be alive and in the hotel, otherwise, why the need for identification? We stepped out into the lobby, and it was otherworldly. It was so hard to believe that it was the same lobby I had walked through eighteen hours before to head up to my hotel room and take a nap.

It looked like a movie set after a very intense battle scene. Every, single pane of glass had been broken. Every single one. And the remaining shards of glass, just as they had been upstairs, were everywhere. There was a bit of smoke still hovering in the lobby from all the explosions and gunfire. It looked dystopian as hell. I was surprised as I looked around that I didn't see any bodies, or anything that was obviously blood. I wondered, briefly, if they had cleaned up the lobby a little to make it so that the survivors could stomach it as they walked through. I was trying to process that it really was the same place as they walked me over to a couch where there were more American men waiting. They hoisted me onto the cushions as I looked around in total shock, shaking. We were surrounded in a massive ring by Kenyan Special Forces guys. I started sobbing, looking at each of them in turn and saying, "Thank you, thank you, thank you." None responded, they were focused on the situation around them, and I was thankful for that, too. Then Carter and Sam told me they were going to go get the 'other American.' Another American! Who was still alive?! Amazing! I was so happy that there was another life to be saved. They hustled off and I thought of the imminent comfort that person was to feel, and it warmed my exhausted heart.

12 weeks ATA: I can't go to the shooting range. It's so crazy. We used to go sometimes. Not often, but sometimes, and I liked it, I liked how powerful I felt when I would hold a gun, when I would shoot through the bullseye on the target even though it was as far away as the settings would allow. I liked to feel the reverberation in my hands, that kick that went all the way up into my shoulders when I would pull the

trigger. I liked to learn, to get better, to feel like I was improving, getting more accurate. And that was when I didn't even believe in allowing guns into my house. They were for the shooting range only, for sport, and not for a home. Now all I want is to sleep curled up next to a loaded fucking pistol, and yet I cannot bring myself to return to the shooting range. Paul keeps asking me to go; I think he is aware that I am avoiding it, but I keep making excuses. I can't go there. All I can think is that it must be sheer idiocy to put yourself, voluntarily, into a room of strangers with guns. Strangers are scary and unpredictable, and they likely have nefarious intentions. And then to stand right next to them as they hold weapons in their hands that can eradicate your life in the blink of an eye? No fucking thank you. It just feels like I would be asking to get killed. It's wild. It's like I gained a belief in guns but lost my faith in strangers.

Another of the American guys took the place of Sam and Carter next to me on the couch. He was massive, I felt like he had to be as big as a house! And so strong. He asked if he could get me some water, but I thanked him and declined. I wanted him to stay right next to me. I wanted all of them to stay next to me. I asked him, hesitantly, if it was really safe to just sit in the lobby like this, even though rationally I knew that I wouldn't be sitting there if it wasn't safe. I just wanted to hear him say it. He assured me that it was indeed safe, at which point something inside me just broke open. I leaned into his shoulder and started sobbing, without saying any words or giving any sort of explanation. I didn't even know his name. I was just so goddamn overwhelmed and exhausted and thankful and terrified all at once. He stiffened, and then gave me this super awkward pat on the back, at which point I nearly laughed as I realized that I had made him uncomfortable! This incredibly brave man who was in the lobby of an active terrorist attack was uncomfortable trying to comfort a sobbing woman! I leaned backward off of him, and he again offered to get me a water bottle. Since it seemed like he needed to do it more than I needed him to do it, I thanked him and said that would be great. He went behind the bar in the little lounge attached to the lobby, and he took a bottle of water out of the refrigerator. It was insane. He brought me an in-tact glass water bottle with the hotel's logo on it. It was hard to believe that this was a glass structure that somehow had not been destroyed in the mayhem. It was even harder to believe that I could just sit on that couch and drink it in total comfortable safety. That no part of me needed to wonder if I should smash it and save the pieces of glass in case I needed to kill myself. Somehow some combination of these amazing, brave men all around me had taken away that possibility in my life. In fact, they had given me back my life.

It's March 4, so almost 2 months ATA, and only today did I deeply and truly realize I'm going to be ok. Until now, I never believed it.

Then I jumped: the text! That last text I had sent my family was so ambiguous! Oh my god, they might have thought I meant that the *bad* guys had gotten me! I started to pull my phone out of my pocket, but then realized I shouldn't startle all of these soldiers. I looked at the one closest to me and asked if I could please send my family a text to let them know I was safe. He nodded. I opened my phone to see an instant reply from my dad: "Who!? Who got you!?" Paul, in his infinite wisdom had responded, "I am sure she means the good guys. That's great!" I added to his explanation, saying that yes indeed it was the good guys, and I was out of the hotel room and would contact them as soon as I could. But I still couldn't internalize it, even as I said it to them. Could it really be true? Was it over? Was I really safe? And then the most amazing thing happened. One of the Kenyan Special Forces guys held up a cell phone and started playing the Star Wars victory song at top volume. The other guys encircled him, laughing and high fiving. And while I never would have thought that I could have laughed while I was still inside that god-forsaken hotel, I almost did. Because it was so clear that they were celebrating. That we should all be celebrating. Because we had won. The good guys had won. We were victorious, and we were going to live.

You know what one of the most fucked up things is that I feel ATA? A deep sense of empathy for the men. The terrorists. I cry sometimes, thinking about how unnecessary it was for them to lose their lives. How unnecessary it was for them to take the lives of twenty-one innocent people. How differently their lives could have turned out if they had had love and support and access to resources and education. If they had known good men and women who had taken care of them. If they hadn't fallen prey to an extremist group with an agenda. Because ultimately, like us, they were just pawns that day in Al Shabaab's statement to the Kenyan government, and like so many victims in the hotel, it cost them their lives. But these were men who were willing to sacrifice themselves for what they believed in. They had to know they were never coming back out of the hotel alive, but they went in anyway. That's how much they believed in their cause. But what they couldn't see was that they had been tricked. Their cause was twisted and sick and wrong. They gave their lives for something deeply horrific, because they were misled. If only their lives had gone differently. They could have proudly served in the army of their country. They could have moved to America and proudly served in ours. And we could have avoided all that senseless death that day. We could have saved so many lives, we could have saved so much of our own humanity.

Carter and Sam came back right about then with the other American victim, and he introduced himself to me as Tim. He was completely calm, and I almost laughed, thinking that he was really making me look bad! He asked me how I was doing as one of the burly Americans hustled off to, of course, get him some water. I told him that I was ok, and asked him, almost incredulous at his demeanor, how he was doing. He said that other than a foot injury (which predated the attack) he was doing fine. My eyes were so large as I stared at him, practically popping out of my head as I wondered how the hell he was so calm, so nonchalant about all of this. The big American guy returned and handed him a bottle of water, and then it was time, finally fucking time, to actually leave the property. As I turned toward the covered entrance to the lobby where my driver had dropped me off eighteen hours before, where usually the employees stood in their feathered hats screening bags and running a detection wand over the people entering, I saw an armored vehicle that was waiting for us. Carter and Sam and the other American guys walked us out to the vehicle, tossed our bags in the back, got us situated, and then hopped in. As we drove out, off of that property and out of the terrorist attack, never to return, there was only one thing I could think to say: "It's a good goddamn day to be an American."

Part Five: Salvation

As we pulled out onto the road into the streaming sunshine that burned on, as it does, regardless of the trials and tribulations of our unimportant species, I turned to Tim. He was still incredibly calm, and he was looking out the window as if this was simply another Uber ride in a safe neighborhood. I tapped him on the arm. I had to know. "Tim," I started, then waited. I wasn't sure how to ask it exactly. Finally I said, "Do you think we will always remember this as the best day of our lives, or the worst?" He didn't even hesitate. "Both." He said it calmly, self-assuredly. It was like he was a terrorist attack pro, no nerves, no concerns, and he already knew exactly how we would process it. I think back on that moment all the time. It is amazing to me just how right he was.

18 weeks ATA: I am compiling this book just over four months ATA. I still have really hard days. I still have really great days. Some days I make progress, some days I can't get off the couch. I can go to gyms and grocery stores again but setting foot inside a hotel still brings on a panic attack. But at least these days I know I will get there. And I spend a lot of time thinking about the fact that BTA, I looked like I had it all, at least on the surface. But I didn't feel fulfilled. I desperately wanted to find a career that let me help people full time. I wanted to be an author, with a published book on the shelves of bookstores. When I was at my cubicle, I would find myself dreaming about those things, and I would try to push them away and talk myself into being content without them. And believe me, the irony of the fact that the attack gave me those things is not lost on me. Or perhaps I took them from the attack, as I salvaged my life and put myself back together. I don't know. Mostly, I just feel thankful that I have the opportunity to take the worst day of my life and begin a conversation about PTSD and soldiers and pain and healing that I believe really needs to happen.

A little way off the property, there was a barricade, and then a ton of parked cars and I think some news vehicles were there too. At first it seemed insane that anyone would voluntarily be close to that hotel, to the scene of that horror, but then I realized that many people were probably waiting for loved ones. That's where I would be if someone I loved had been trapped in that hell for seventeen hours. I started looking into their faces through the tinted glass of the armored vehicle, hoping that each person I looked upon would have their loved one returned to them safe and sound. Then I saw a face among the crowd that I recognized! It was my driver, who had dropped me not so far from there the previous morning. We locked eyes and he started waving and gesturing wildly, as I searched in vain for a way to roll down my window. I started shouting to the guys in the front that I knew that man, that I had texted him from inside the hotel, and begging them to roll down my window so I could tell him I was ok. They slowed the vehicle to give me a moment to return his gestures, but also informed me there was no way to do so, that would compromise the integrity and security of the vehicle. I gave him a huge smile and two thumbs up through the tinted glass, and he smiled his beautiful big smile back at me, looking relieved. I grabbed my phone and started texting him that I was ok, and thanking him for being there, waiting for me. He told me that he had waited all night, and that he wasn't going to leave until he knew I was ok. He had been there for over twelve hours, waiting to see if a girl he had known for two days would make it out alive. I thanked him profusely. I wanted to hug him. He was the only one in that entire country that I knew remotely well. The only one who had waited for me amongst loved ones of the other victims. And had the Americans not extracted me, he would have been the shoulder that I would've cried on. Stranger is a strange term in circumstances like that. He was, in so many ways as he stood there smiling, my connection back to humanity. I cried, tiny, happy tears, as we drove away from him.

3 weeks ATA: Some days I realize the memory is getting hazier, further away. Time really does heal all things I guess, or at least dull all things. I feel better, less frenzied, less terrified, the more time passes. It feels less close to me, less like a real memory and more like a terrible movie. I no longer hear the sound of the explosion ringing in my ears when I try to go to sleep. I no longer remember exactly the words I exchanged with my family when the gunshots started, just sort of a summary. I no longer feel the chilly tile of the bathroom floor against my feet, my arms, my back, my face. So even on the days when I can't get off the couch, I find solace in the fact that every single day puts more distance between me and the attack.

I didn't know where we were going, and I hadn't bothered to ask. I wanted to stay with these men for as long as they would let me. I was secretly wishing they would take us straight to a hangar, where they would board a plane with us and stay by our sides all the way back to the US. But then, in the middle of the street, we pulled over and stopped. I started to panic, asking desperately what the hell was going on. I looked out the tinted windows but saw only a huge gate that we had parked parallel to, not perpendicular as if we planned to enter it. Looking more closely I realized it was a gate outside of a residential or business complex, but it didn't look official or government-owned. Suddenly two other men had appeared outside our vehicle, also wearing bulletproof vests, but theirs had "FBI" emblazoned on the front. As they opened our doors, they told us they needed to ask us a few questions. They asked us, politely, to step out of the vehicle. I didn't want to, I never wanted to be outdoors again, I wanted to go directly to a fucking airplane and not step outside until I was back on sweet, American soil, but they were calm and insistent, and I was too tired to put up any resistance. Plus, of course, Tim was behaving and being super obedient, so throwing a fit and refusing to get out of the car would have looked ridiculous. The FBI guys were calm, their voices kind. They asked if I needed to sit, but I said that no, I could stand. They asked repeatedly if I had sustained any injuries, even small ones, and I assured them again and again that I had not. They searched my body and clothes for any blood, worried that my shock might be keeping me from realizing I had been injured, but they eventually concluded I really was, physically at least, ok. Carter and Sam again materialized next to us, and offered us water bottles, which actually made me laugh out loud. What was with all the water bottles?! Were we stocking up for something I didn't know about? I declined politely saying I already had a bottle of water, and they looked crestfallen. Then one of them, I can't remember which one, perked up and offered me a soda. But when I said I don't drink soda, the crestfallen look returned. Again, I felt they needed to bring me a beverage more than I needed to consume it, so I said that on second thought I would love another water, and they ran off to grab it (from I don't even know where that time). In the meantime, one of the FBI guys, whose names I don't think I ever caught, stepped in and started asking me every routine question you can think of. Name, address, parents' names and addresses, maiden names, where I was born, where they were born, etc. Even in the moment, I was thankful that all those things were so burned into my brain, because I was running on less than fumes. Any answers that didn't come as second nature would have been impossible to come up with at all. I stood there, answering him, standing in the dust on the side of the road, and then some movement behind the gate caught my eye. The FBI guy had asked if I still happened to have my passport, which I gave him, and as he took it somewhere to examine it, I just stood there, staring at the gate. There were all these faces pressed right up against the bars, staring at us from inside. Staring at the Americans Who Lived. At the men from the best military in the world. And my first instinct was panic, wondering if these strangers, too, wanted us dead. They didn't look particularly sympathetic, only deeply serious. When the FBI guy came back and said he had verified our identities and we could now hop in his vehicle and proceed to the Embassy, I was immensely relieved. I hated being stared at like that. It was the first moment that my new life set in. It was the first moment where I realized that I had become a spectacle.

I think about that med eval all the time. I think about the Kenyans who live there, permanently. They had looked out at us through the bars, and the intense and serious looks on their faces worried me. I wasn't convinced we were safe with all these emotionless faces staring out at us from between those bars. But I didn't think about how close they'd come. How close they'd continue to come. I didn't know then that the majority of those who died that day were Kenyan and these strangers were just lucky that that particular attack was not on their place of work. But the next one could be. I was going to get the hell out of that country and never look back. They couldn't. Perhaps what I had interpreted as lack of emotion was actually fear. Perhaps in that moment, we had so much more in common than I realized. Perhaps I had been too quick to judge them, to label them as dangerous and want to get away from them, when really, we could have forged a bond. They understood my terror far better than my friends and family in the US ever could. And they weren't the only ones. So many people, all around the world, live in that fear and terror every day, and in some places it's even more acute than in Kenya, and I was now bonded to them irrevocably. Perhaps I should take that lesson and carry it very close to me, to ensure that the fear doesn't get away from me. Because isn't that exactly what the terrorists want? They want us to tear ourselves apart, to ignore our similarities and self-implode because of perceived differences. It is in separation and war that terrorists can gain footing. But we have to outsmart them, outsmart that sort of terror. We have to swallow it down and see our similarities. Find ways to come together. Because that will be our only salvation.

I didn't realize it at the time, but at that med eval and identity check Carter and Sam, the guys who pulled us out, who physically removed us from that horrific scene, disappeared. I have never seen them since, but I think about them every single day. Perhaps Tim noticed, because he asked a question about military operations in Africa, about whether the Americans had been able to take charge when they showed up, or what the rules of engagement looked like in a foreign country. The answer made me laugh. The FBI driver hesitated, then said he couldn't get into it, but what he could tell us was that this was Africa. After a pause, where I think he internalized the fact that Tim and I had no idea what that meant, he clarified by saying that the Kenyan Special Forces had, thankfully, openly welcomed assistance. He wrapped up with a single phrase: "There are no straight lines here." I thought it was a great description. And it reminded me, for just a moment, of all the beauty I had seen in that country the day and a half before the attack. Of the baby elephant sanctuary I had visited just the morning before, the giraffes I had fed by hand, the amazing food I had tasted, and the beautiful, resilient people who had built homes and schools and churches out of corrugated metal sheets, into which they had welcomed me with open arms. Of the twin boys I had played hide and seek with, even though none of us spoke a word of the other's language. It reminded me of how much more that country is than the site of these terrorist attacks. Of how Kenyans had died right next to Westerners in that hotel over the last day. And that really was the only way to describe it all. No straight lines.

1 week ATA: I have no idea what I need. Everyone asks me what I need, what they can do. If I knew, I would tell them, but I have never been through a terrorist attack before, I am not seasoned in knowing how to deal with it. I just take my best guess, which is inevitably wrong. I told my friends to treat me totally normally, as if nothing had happened. I told them I didn't want to dwell on what had happened. Then I found myself furious when they treated me the same way as always; I felt like they were forgetting about the attack, like they didn't care what I was going through. Carolyn says what I need will change constantly, and I will just have to update everyone as it changes. But that sounds exhausting. And I am already so tired all the time. So I just turn my phone off instead.

I still think about Tim a lot, too. In his own way, he was a hero that day also, at least to me. I think he could see how shaken I was, how much I was still afraid. So he started telling a great story, one that I have reiterated to my friends and family and which we still quote all the time. He said he has a wife and two kids back home, and his wife has a funny and rather dry sarcastic sense of humor. He said that last year, they had bought a bunch of chickens, which lived on their property and which their kids had absolutely fallen in love with. But then one day a weird bout of some sort of chicken illness had struck, and all of the chickens had been left dead in its wake. Worrying that plague was a bit of a scary and intense topic for their two young children, he and his wife had decided to just get rid of the bodies and tell the kids that the chickens had fallen ill and so they were at the vet. Whenever the kids would remember to ask about the chickens, first every few days, then every few weeks, then every few months, he and his wife would just assure them that the chickens were still with the vet. He laughed as he told me that they had known it wasn't the best long-term plan, but it was working in the short term at least. So he explained that when he had started texting his wife from his hotel room on the second floor, where he too had been trapped for seventeen hours but which, thankfully, was on the far side of the hotel so he had never seen the exploded body or the men with guns, his wife had responded something like, "You better not die, Tim! The kids will never believe me that you are at the vet, too!"

12 weeks ATA: I just read Mallory Smith's book, Salt in my Soul. If I can ever write something that can impact a single person the way that just impacted me, my entire life will feel worth it, not to mention my experience in January. I wish I had known Mallory, and I wish more than anything that I could thank her for her profound words. To read her private journal entries, to hear her describe in such personal words and personal detail what it was like to face a chronic illness, one that gave her a considerably shortened lifespan, to face

*that every day with such courage and grace, and still man-
age to talk about how thankful she was for her illness because of the bettered perspectives it gave her, it blew my
mind. If she could live with her diagnosis and still be such an
inspiration, then I at least know that I can make it through
this. And maybe, just maybe, I can be better for it, and realize my lifelong dream of publishing a book and helping people, just like she did. It's best said in her words, "Being frustrated and angry that something was taken from you hurts
creativity, the very same creativity that could help you rein-
vent your possibilities and achieve your ends."*

Tim kept me entertained the rest of the drive to the
Embassy, but as we pulled up, some of my anxiety and
fear returned. The building looked tranquil enough, but
that also made it feel, at least to me, like it was an easy
target. If the terrorists had planned some sort of coordi-
nated attack, wasn't the Embassy naturally going to be
included? Had they already had a suicide bomber infil-
trate the premises somehow? Were more gunmen on the
way? I didn't know it in the moment, but my brain had
been retrained to expect danger anywhere I had previously felt safe. It was something that would take me months
of therapy and dozens and dozens of hours of homework
to start to fix. I voiced my concerns to the FBI guys as
they helped us out of the vehicles and grabbed our bags,
but they nearly laughed in response. They assured me
that the Embassy was practically a bunker, impenetrable
and more than safe. The safest place, perhaps, in the
whole city at that instant. That they had stepped up all
security and even added extra military protection and
guards. I wasn't completely reassured, but I sure as fuck

wasn't about to wait in the parking lot so I followed them inside. I realized, then, that there was a pre-established procedure they had to follow with victims like us. They explained that we would have to have a medical evaluation, then a psychological one, then a formal debrief about what we saw and heard, and then we could get some time to rest, talk to our families, and figure out a plan to get the hell off the continent.

16 weeks ATA: Avoidance is so comfortable. Healing is not. I can't even tell you how much I just want to avoid this bullshit. I want to get back to my life, get back to being myself. And I can't do that if I am listening to myself talk about the worst thing that ever happened to me on repeat! I can't do it if I am exhausted and introverted. I can't do it if I wear out after an hour of conversation. I am done! I feel better, isn't that the point of therapy? I feel better, I can go to restaurants without too much concern, I can go to big box stores, and even, sometimes in smaller towns, shopping malls. I don't need much more than this. I don't need to be able to go to hotels. I don't need to be able to think about or talk about what happened in January. I am ok. I have processed the trauma! I just want to be done. I want to erase all the recordings and never go back to therapy and get back to my life. I am better. Right? How the hell do you know if you're better?

For me, med was quick. Once again, I was proven correct in that I had not sustained any physical injuries, just mental ones. Tim's medical check took a lot longer because of his foot injury, another hilarious story that he would tell me in a few hours. In my psych check, I wasn't sure what I was supposed to say. I was so tired I was literally swaying on my feet, so she brought me a chair, and then asked me a bunch of routine but absolutely ridiculous questions. She asked if I had any urges to kill myself, harm anyone else, or drink. I told her that all I really wanted to do at that instant was sleep, in particular I was wishing I was next to the fireplace at my parents' home in Ohio, safe and sound and sleeping next to the crackling fire. She told me that was good. Then she asked if I wanted to talk about anything I had seen or experienced in the attack. I told her that what stood out most was that I hadn't wished I could change my life. I didn't have any epiphanies about getting a new job or new fiancé or moving or anything like that. I had simply realized that I deeply loved my life, and mostly my people, my family and Paul, and that I had so desperately wanted to marry that amazing man. And so at that moment, as I looked into her bright, light eyes, and explained to her, out loud, that now I was going to get to marry that man after all, it sunk in, just a little, that it was true. That I was going to see all those people again. Hug them. Tell them, to their faces, how much I love them. Walk down the aisle with Paul. Marry the man of my dreams. And it was the most beautiful realization I have ever had in my life.

18 weeks ATA: Prolonged exposure really does suck. More than I can put into words. But it also works. You take the memories that haunt you, the very worst ones, that pop up in your dreams and in front of your eyes throughout the day, the ones that truly torment you, and you pull them out and look directly at them. You do not try to hide from them or keep them at bay. You listen to them over and over and over, and by doing so, you wear them down. Like an old quilt that you wear down until it's threadbare, and it becomes merely a shadow of what it used to be. That's what you do to the memories of the trauma. Do you have any childhood memories that you cherished, but you've thought of them or talked about them so many times that you almost remember remembering them more than actually experiencing them? So the memory has lost its lifelike qualities and become lackluster? It becomes hard to remember some of the pieces that you used to know, the colors dull, and the characters fade. You become confused about some of the particulars. It's like that, but with a terrible memory, and you do it on purpose, though rather against your own will. And it's terribly painful. Imagine listening to yourself describe, in sobs, the worst thing that has ever happened to you. Your heart starts racing, and your hands shake, and tears roll down your cheeks uninhibited. You are seeing every terrible detail right in front of your eyes all over again. You are back on that bathroom floor saying goodbye to your loved ones. Then when it ends, imagine trying to leave your apartment and make small talk or chat with your friends. It makes living the rest of your life immensely difficult. But the upside is that those memories cannot take you by surprise anymore when you've faced them by choice time and time again. It really is just like the broken leg. You won't heal completely unless you do the physical therapy. Which sucks and is painful and draining. But you have to remember why you're doing it. That's how it is with PE. I never want to listen to my recordings. But instead, I remind myself why I want to get better. That I want to get better for Paul and my parents and my brother. I want to be able to work again. I want to be able to go to restaurants again. I want to have so much capacity

in my reservoir that I can be there for all my friends. I want
to sleep again. I want, so badly, to get better. I give myself
that little pep talk, and then I put the recording on. It's ter-
rible and I cry and I wince and it wears me out completely.
But for the rest of that day, I am free. I controlled the memo-
ry, instead of letting it control me. And in trauma recovery,
little victories are everything.

Tim caught my eye at some point when we were waiting between stations, before our FBI debrief. There were a
few minutes where we were being handed off, from one
escort to another, so we were standing by ourselves in the
hallway waiting for another person to grab us and take us
wherever we had to go next. He raised his eyebrows excitedly and said, "How cool is it that it was Navy SEALs
who pulled us out?!" The question caught me remarkably
off guard. Who was he talking about? The Embassy guys?
The incredibly strong, calm, businesslike Embassy guys,
who were very nonchalant about the whole thing... Almost
as if they had been trained for really hardcore evacuation
situations...Almost as if they had experienced many situations just like ours before and there was nothing all that
surprising about it... The guys who had set up a security
outpost at the front desk when the hotel was still being
blown up... The guys who had told me 'not to worry'
about who they were with... It finally clicked. Of course
those hadn't just been guys who usually sit at a desk in
the Embassy! Plus, I had been told there were reports of
US and UK Special Operations Forces on the ground. And
they had come and extracted the Americans, ensured that
we were safely handed off and taken to the Embassy, far
out of harm's way. I started crying. In what world are you

on the other side of the fucking planet and the Navy SEALs come pull you out of a terrorist attack?! I had never felt gratitude or patriotism that acutely before. I wanted to find them one last time and thank them again, now that I knew and understood who they really were. Now that I had digested the fact that Tim and I were probably not the only people they had saved or would save in the future. Now that I knew that their *career choice* had been to go into dangerous situations like that and rescue strangers. My awe at their bravery cemented itself even more firmly in my mind. Then I started laughing, maybe that also explained the water bottle thing! Presumably these guys had done hundreds of hours of training on victim extraction from a hostage situation, but how much training had been provided on what to do with the victims once you had them? Maybe the entirety of that module was: check them for physical injuries that need immediate attention, get them to hydrate, and hand them off. So when I didn't have injuries and I didn't need water, they were at a loss! I laughed to myself, and then my laughter turned to tears. I was so overwhelmed with emotion. And I still think of them all the time, and that bravery they possess which I can't even fathom. I still cry, too, thinking of how amazing it is that I was extracted by some of the most badass guys around, the Navy fucking SEALs. (While I'm incredibly thankful for these men and everything they've given to me and our country, I would later learn that they likely weren't SEALs, and hadn't been directly involved in the action that day. The man who had wouldn't be revealed to me for almost a year.)

1 week ATA: Carolyn asks me how I feel, and I tell her I

feel defeated. I feel like I lost things, pieces of me, in that attack that I will never get back. And I am so overwhelmingly sad about it, because I didn't realize it at first. At first, I just assumed I was still whole. She pauses, then she asks me what I want to feel like when therapy is over. When I am 'better,' totally 'healed.' It takes me a long time to answer. I run through a lot of words in my head, wondering if it's whole or normal that I want to feel, but those aren't right. I know I may never feel those things again, so I shouldn't set them as my goal. Then it occurs to me, the perfect word. "Victorious." I say. I want to feel like ultimately the victory that day goes not to the terrorists, not even just to the SEALs, SAS and KSF, but also to me, to all the victims who lived. That we all feel like we weren't just left broken and defeated, but that ultimately, we triumphed. We came out more resilient and more badass than ever. I don't just want to go back to 'normal.' I want to be even better.

My memories from the Embassy, like my memories from the hotel room, are blurry and often missing some detail. I can see some scenes extremely clearly, and some are harder to recall, more distant, blurred by what was at that point overwhelming exhaustion. At some point in the Embassy, I realized that I hadn't slept in over forty hours. Things were often dreamlike, distant from me even as I was living them, not to mention the fact that I was alive at all seemed surreal, hard to believe. Here are some of the scenes I remember very clearly. At some point a man was escorting me between stops, perhaps medical and psych, or psych and my debrief, I am not sure. He was not FBI, just an employee of the Embassy, but he was American. He was, as most of the employees tried to do, attempting to make small talk, a bizarre custom given the gravity of the preceding hours, but I appreciated the attempt all the same. He asked how I was holding up, and then doubled back and asked my name. I told him and his face lit up completely. "You're Meyli?!" He said excitedly. When I nodded, he continued, "I love your name! It's so unique!" I was thrown off by his exuberance, everyone else, myself included, was feeling rather somber. I looked at him, bemused, without saying anything, and he added, "Do you know how many Meyli Chapins there are?? Just the one! Just you! Do you know how many Tim Smiths there are? Even just in Georgia?! Tons! But there is only one you. We have had your name and identification since six pm last night!" He said this last part proudly, as if he was expecting a high five or some sort of congratulations. I just stared at the floor, my brain doing the math. My only thought was: I had already been on the bathroom floor for three painstaking, terrifying hours by six pm last night. What the fuck took them so goddamn long? I chose not to say anything at all.

14 weeks ATA: Last week was hard and terrible. I was irritable and snappy, which made me guilty and thereby even more miserable in a relentless cycle. It was the first time since I've been back that I really wanted to die. It's been so hard to find meaning in anything. And I keep so much bottled up. I worry that this is just who I am now, and it kills me. It doesn't feel like a life worth living. But Paul, saint that he is, just continues to put up with me. And Dahlia, saint that she is, said all the right things in our session. She kindly and patiently reminded me that I will get better, that PTSD is normal, and more importantly it's transient, which means it does not (or at least won't continue to) define me. She says it won't feel like this forever, that I will get to the post traumatic growth (PTG) stage, and my battle against PTSD will ultimately end up giving me experiences that I can use to help others. I told her that if that's really true, if I can use this hell to better the lives of others, then all this horror (during and after the attack) will have been worth it. At least that's a life that's beautifully meaningful. I want so badly to get better, because I want to want to live that life.

Later, a really polite and wonderful gentleman who worked at the Embassy offered to take us for lunch. Tim declined, I think due to the ever-increasing pain in his foot, but I realized when he offered that I was absolutely starving. My last real meal had been about twenty-four hours beforehand. He took me down to the cafe, and then asked if I wanted to sit outside or inside. I thought that was an insane question, who the hell would want to sit outside to eat? That's how people fucking die. I said inside, please. He bought my lunch, and then started on the same painful strain of attempted small talk, but he sensed my unwillingness to chat and carried the effort of the conversation himself, which I appreciated. He told me about his job, and about working to undermine the terrorist threat in Kenya and what a difficult job that is. Then he said something that almost made me sick. "We stop so many, one has to slip through every once in a while." I know that even in the moment he didn't realize what a crass thing that was to say, or how upsetting it would be to someone who had barely lived through the 'one that had slipped through.' He really was kind and sympathetic and overall I enjoyed lunch with him. But sometimes when I can't sleep, I still hear him saying that phrase over and over. Every once in a while, one has to slip through.

Everyone asks me: what's the right thing to say to a trauma survivor? But there isn't a right thing. There was no right thing to say to me. No one could fix what I was going through. None of my friends could stop my nightmares or flashbacks. But there was deep comfort in knowing that people were there to lean on. That even if I wasn't reaching out to them, I could. Even if I wasn't letting them in, or telling them what was going on, they'd listen if I chose to. So stop getting caught up in what to say to someone you know who has gone through something horrible and just say something. Just reach out. Say you don't know what to say, but you are there for them. Because that could make all the difference.

The US Embassy in Nairobi really is rather like a bunker. It has these massive doors with bolts that slide in and out automatically when a code is entered or an identification card is read. They are extremely loud, and the doors are immensely heavy, which adds to the noise because they are forever slamming. I jumped every, single time I heard a door, for all ten hours I was there. I wanted to run or scream, I kept thinking every sound the doors made was an explosion. I kept thinking, "They're here!" I also would try to calm myself down, tell myself that it was just leftover adrenaline. That I needed sleep, and a good meal and a nice bed and a hug from my family and all of this intensity, all these blood-curdling, automatic responses would fade. I was wrong. My brain had been reprogrammed for seventeen hours to believe that all loud noises were dangerous. All loud noises signaled a potential violent end to my life. Even if I was in a place I previously believed was safe. When I would eventually get back to the US, I would realize that I could no longer frequent grocery stores or gyms or restaurants or hair salons or schools or work. Anywhere with doors that could slam. Anywhere without immediate access to the exit. Because fight or flight mode doesn't just turn off when you live through something terrible. It becomes second nature, overly accessible, kicking into overdrive all the time, with or without your consent. It's your brain, trying to protect you, but ultimately making your life unlivable.

4 weeks ATA: Google HR started texting me last week. Not my work phone, my personal phone. It made me jump. I didn't want them texting me, didn't want people who couldn't spell my name right to text me about the worst day of my life. I wanted them to go away, to let me take 'as much time' as I needed, as they had initially told me I could do. But last week, they started saying I have to go out on official leave. They gave me the email address of some woman who would help me do so. When I emailed that woman, she had no idea who I was or what had happened. She sent me links and long forms, and she could not answer my questions about how I was supposed to fill them out. She told me that "it is Google's policy that you will not receive leave pay until your claim has been approved..." So she could not help me fill out these forms, she could not tell me if Dahlia was able to fill them out as the 'physician' required to sign off on them, and she could not tell me if my claim would be approved, but she could tell me that as soon as I requested leave, I would stop being paid. The rage subsided, replaced

with a feeling of defeat mixed with something else, some-
thing cold, I think I would call it doubt. I started to feel like I
was crazy. Google was treating me as if this was no big deal.
As if they had no extra responsibility to me, or to help me get
what I needed, even though I had been caught in that terror-
ist attack because I was staying in the 'security-assessed' ho-
tel that they had recommended, while I was on a business
trip for them. Maybe I was just wrong. Maybe I was assum-
ing too much. Maybe I did not deserve extra help or treat-
ment. Maybe I was blowing this all out of proportion in my
head, when any objective third party would agree it was not
a big deal at all. I honestly didn't know. I had always trusted
Google, I had recruited for them, telling people things like,
"They're not like other big companies. They care about you
as a person." Now here I was, needing them to care about me
as a person, but getting nothing. In fact, Dahlia told me to-
day that my interactions with them are actually exacerbat-
ing my PTSD. And yet, they seem completely unmoved. They
are checking boxes, passing me off to the next person and the
next, telling me to fill out forms and cross my fingers that I
am granted leave. Is that right? Is that what I deserve from
them after three years and one terrorist attack? I don't
know. I don't know anything anymore.

Two other things were regular occurrences during
those ten hours in the Embassy. The first was that people
would say, in passing, that at least I now had a 'great story
for the grandkids.' It was one of the worst things to say. It
was far too soon to talk about what happened in that hotel being a good story. It was too soon to make light of it
or talk about it as if it was far away, a faded memory I
could relate, without pain, to grandkids. It was all still

way too close and way too scary. I still frown when people say that about anything to this day. I don't recommend that line for trauma survivors. The other was that we would get standing ovations and sympathetic looks from little cubicles of strangers, American, Kenyan and otherwise. But I felt we didn't deserve applause, in fact it was confusing, startling even. I kept looking around to see who they were clapping for, and then realizing that it was for me and Tim. But we had lived due to pure random chance and the heroic acts of strangers, not through anything we had personally done. Applause seemed so very bizarre and unfitting. I kept hesitating, not sure whether to clap for them in return, or stare at them, or thank them, or just walk by as if it wasn't happening. I appreciated that it was a kind gesture, but in my state of dreamlike unreality, I mostly went with the latter.

5 weeks ATA: My apartment building is under construction. It's like a sick joke. I already am barely able to get a few hours of sleep each night, and now I wake in a full panic to electric tools slamming on the walls, and men shouting at the top of their lungs in a foreign language. I have panic attacks regularly because of the noise, and I can't sleep on Sunday nights because I know the beautiful silence of the weekend is over and they will return in the morning. I feel enraged all the time, enraged that our landlord can reconstruct the building we live in without giving us the option to move, enraged at the timing of it all, enraged that I cannot control my rage. Which leads me to a feeling of impotence, and then immense depression. Which joins with all the other rage and depression I am already feeling, and threatens to overwhelm me completely. If we don't get out of here soon, I honestly don't know what I will do. I worry constantly that one day the depression will get the best of me, and I will be seized by the idea that I should just end it all, I should just take my own life. It would be so quick and so easy.

Before my FBI debrief, they asked if there was anything I needed to do first. I said that actually there was: I was desperate to brush my teeth. It had been over a day since I had been able to do so, and all the panting and crying and hyperventilating and fasting had really done a number on my breath and the inside of my mouth. It made talking to all those strangers considerably more uncomfortable because I was always trying to lean away from them to spare them the smell of my breath. The inside of my mouth felt almost fuzzy, half from the dehydration and lack of food, and half from the need to brush my teeth. The FBI guys were apologetic, seeming to feel bad they hadn't thought to give us a moment to clean up. Tim joked that brushing his teeth wouldn't be enough for him, he was stinky and sweaty head to toe, and when he said that I realized that I was too. I had sweat so much in those seventeen hours because of the terror and adrenaline, it had soaked all the way through everything I was wearing. I became acutely aware of the odor on my clothes and body in that moment. And, embarrassed as I was, I was mostly just excited. Excited that I could care about something like brushing my teeth or changing my clothes again. Excited that, with my life secured, I could care about those mundane, unimportant details, like keeping my bad breath away from strangers. It was an awesome moment. One of the lovely women who had been helping to escort me around all day took me to the bathroom and let me scrub and scrub and scrub at my teeth. I nearly jumped out of my skin at one point when someone closed a stall door so hard that it slammed, but still I was happy as I stood there, looking in the mirror, smiling lips covered in toothpaste foam, alive as could be.

16 weeks ATA: I was at a wedding today, a family member was getting married, my cousin. So there were tons of relatives there, and I had been wary to attend in the first place because I really didn't want to have all these distant cousins asking me all the morbid questions they could come up with about what happened in January. But it wasn't like that at all; people were polite, a little standoffish if anything, which honestly, I appreciated. And I spent most of the time shielded by Paul, my parents and my brother which was fantastic. And then, toward the end of the night, the song Footloose came on, which is always one of my mom's favorites. She is a dancer by training, but she is also just kooky as hell and an absolute blast. She dragged me out onto the dance floor with her, a huge smile on her face, and then started dancing away, doing the steps from the movie. People around her were smiling and laughing; there is always a crowd around my mom when she is on the dance floor. And for a moment I felt like I was above the whole scene looking down. And I could see this amazing, joy-filled woman who loves me more than anything. I could see the crowd around her laughing and smiling, her joy absolutely infectious. And I started crying as I stood there, shaking my hips and laughing with her on the dance floor. I started crying these tears of joy that I was with her, in person, holding her hand. That I had not died on a bathroom floor in January. That we were making this memory and that we had so many more smiling memo-

ries left to make. And I hugged her, and all I could think was how lucky I was that I was alive, with a mom like that.

I told the FBI everything I could remember, and they quizzed me about details that didn't match up with other accounts, or videos that were already being posted online. I did my best, but I was so very tired. My desire to tell them anything that could help them catch anyone associated with the horror from the hotel was strong, but it was battling against the fuzziness I was seeing which was caused by lack of sleep. I knew that some of the details were not correct as I was remembering them, or that things were out of chronological order, but I just kept telling them I was doing my best. They were patient and kind, and when they had all the information I could give them they gave me a business card and said to let them know if I remembered any other pertinent details. I left feeling disappointed in myself, that I hadn't paid more attention, hadn't taken any video footage through my window, didn't have any concrete evidence to offer the FBI about who had done this to us. But the disappointment was soon forgotten when I was given the green light to go take a shower. I stayed in the stall for ages, certainly an oddly long time to the folks who were politely waiting for me outside the bathroom (I wasn't allowed to go anywhere in the building unescorted). I just stood in that hot water, enjoying the first physical comfort I had experienced in dozens of hours. Closing my eyes and letting it run over my face, soaking in the noise of the shower which, in addition to the thick bathroom door, drowned out all the scary loud noises. I watched the steam encircle me, and I breathed it in deeply. I thought that maybe I would never get out. But finally, with shriveled fingers, I turned off the water and went to my backpack to see what sort of change of clothes I had packed. That's when I realized that I had another shirt, but no other pants. I thought about washing my reeking, sweat-hardened pants in the sink, but simply could not summon the energy. I put the stinking pants back on and traipsed back out to the hallway to meet my escort. But my warm, clean skin was still an immense comfort.

I went through a progression of songs upon returning that I would listen to at full blast. Songs that seemed to me to capture perfectly what I was feeling. For the first few weeks it was What's Up by 4 Non Blondes, ("I scream from the top of my lungs, 'What's going on?'"). Then You Oughta Know by Alanis Morissette ("It's not fair to deny me the cross I bear that you gave to me"). Then Little Miss by Sugarland ("I'm ok, and it'll be alright again"). And finally, Love Wins by Carrie Underwood ("I believe in the end love wins"). The transitions were not linear, do not misunderstand. I would move to a new song and then feel completely confused and jump back to 4 Non Blondes. But all of these songs now live close to my heart because they provided words for me when I couldn't understand, much less verbalize, how I was feeling, and the fact that they even existed was inherently comforting, because they provided me with concrete evidence that other people in other places had experienced the same feelings I was now experiencing. That is the joy and connection available to us through art.

The woman who was escorting me around took me to an empty office. At my request, she got me access to the internet, and brought my three bottles of water over. I set myself up comfortably in an ergonomic chair at someone's desk; I was told he was traveling that day. Then I got down to business. Through the haze of tiredness I knew I had to do a few things: I had to get a flight the fuck out of there, I had to talk to Paul, and I had to email my boss to tell him I probably wouldn't be back to work for a while (at that time I kept thinking it would be a week, maybe two, but boy was I wrong). I did the first item, then the last, and by that time I had texted Paul and told him I had holed up in an office and could call soon, so he was texting me repeatedly asking when he could call and hear my voice. I was almost scared to talk to him. The shock I was in was comforting, it allowed me to calmly send emails to my boss, respond to all the texts I had gotten that people were praying for me or thinking of me, tell everyone I could that I was alive. But talking to Paul, I worried, would knock the shock away, would expose me completely to the terrifying reality of what had just happened. But I had no choice, he started calling, and it was true that I desperately wanted to hear his voice as well. I answered, and I think he got out a greeting before he completely broke down. This amazing man who had been dead calm all seventeen hours, who had never broken or cried, who had comforted not just me, but as I would later learn had also comforted my parents on a separate thread that whole time, simply lost it. I would have thought that him crying would cause me to sob, but I actually was so caught off guard by him breaking down that it reinforced my calm, my shock. I giggled a little, chiding him that there was no need to cry *now*, now I was very much alive. Now I had a flight booked for that night to head home. Now we needed to get him a flight back to Ohio too, so we could meet there. That in thirty more hours, we would be holding each other. He didn't say much (he never does), he just cried and said he was so happy to hear my voice. I wished with my whole being that we were together in person, wished I could hug him, let him see me, let him touch my face and hold me and content himself that I really was alive. But then I was getting another call, so I asked him to hang on. I switched lines, and it was a voice I would have known anywhere: it was Melissa. She apologized for calling, but said she heard I was out safely and that she just had to hear my voice. For some reason, that one broke me. I started sobbing, and she joined me, and I tried to tell her through the tears over and over that she had been right: she had told me, so many hours before, that I was going to live, I was going to make it out, and here I was. We cried together, half a world apart, for a few minutes that felt like mere seconds, before Paul started calling back, and I hung up with Melissa to spend a bit more time with him. But I still think about that call with Melissa all the time. I still think about how thankful I am for her calm, her pragmatic response to my situation, for telling me to barricade my door and change my shoes and pack a bag. For being a rock to me for so many hours, in the most terrifying time of my entire life, even though we were total strangers. And I say it again here, thank you Melissa.

15 weeks ATA: Today I cried to my therapist, telling her that I feel miserable and guilty all the time. Paul asked me to marry him before I was this broken shell of a person, and now he is not getting what he signed up for. I yell at him for no reason, I am touchy and angry and short-tempered. I don't take care of him at all, I just take from him and he gives and gives. It isn't right and it isn't fair. I told her that I told Paul all of this too and, saint that he is, he just said that was a crazy thing to say, because when he asked me to marry him it was me in any form, and that he was here for the highs and the lows. It was kind of him to say, but it doesn't fix what I am putting him through. Dahlia said something else, though. She told me that PTSD does not define me. It is not my identity, and what I am 'putting Paul through' is entirely made up of PTSD symptoms. The rage, the short temper, the snappiness, the inability to regulate my emotions, the exhaustion, all of these will be alleviated over time. This is why I go to therapy. It's to get my life back. It's to redefine my identity, because PTSD is a temporary condition, it does not define me. I cried tears of joy. It sounds so simple, but I was so lost in this idea that this is who I am now, this terrible, snappy person that doesn't want anyone around and never wants to leave her house. But we talked about how it really is like having a broken limb. When you can't walk on a broken leg, it may be incredibly frustrating, but you still know that when that cast comes off and you do all your physical therapy, one day you will be able to walk on it again. Well that is what Prolonged Exposure is. It's my cast coming off, and physical therapy. It's an absolute bitch most days, but it's how I am going to get better. It's how I am finally going to shake off these symptoms. It's how I am going to be able to feel whole in my relationship again. It's how I am going to redefine myself instead of letting the PTSD do so. I can do this.

The Ambassador wanted to meet us. All the Embassy

employees kept reiterating this to me and Tim, using hushed and reverent whispers as if it was a huge deal. Their eyes were wide, and they would wait for our responses when they told us, as if we would jump up and down with joy and excitement. I have to tell you though, I didn't give a fuck about the US Ambassador to Kenya at the time. I am sure he is a nice guy and all, with a tough job, but he was a stranger to me. I would rather have had Carter and Sam show back up wanting to meet with us, they would have gotten the jumping up and down reaction, at least from me. Those guys actually deserve immense honor, and they'd have received it. This was just some random bureaucrat who wanted to meet us. Once again, I had to get used to my new role as a circus side show. Time to show off the survivors to the boss man. The time in his office was brief and awkward. He told his secretary to 'hold all phone calls' in a very dramatic show of his dedication to giving us his full attention. But when we entered and sat down, there was nothing to say. He told us he was so glad we were alive. We nodded in assent. He told us that it must have been scary. Another nod. He said he was so sorry this had happened. What was there to do besides nod? This continued for a few short moments, then he offered me a tissue, which I took politely and we left. I honestly don't even really remember what he looks like. But hey, I met the US Ambassador to Kenya. I guess it's a cool addition to the story I will have to tell my grandkids.

10 weeks ATA: Another awkward moment that I was avoiding has now arrived and cannot be ignored. I have to see a relative of Paul's relative, a distant, semi-relation who I haven't seen since BTA, who has always been very pleasant, yes, and with whom I like to exchange book recommendations, but we would never have talked about deeply personal things. We would never have talked about life and death. We would never have talked about blood and gore and terrorism and the kind of fear that keeps you from sleeping at night. I don't want to see her, I hate situations like this, where people who were only distantly involved in the periphery of my life before see me now and their eyes fill with tears and they don't know where to look or what to say. But it's also unavoidable. If I don't do it now, I will have to do it later, and what's the point of waiting? I should just get it over with.

But this one time, it's not like I thought it would be. At first, I think I can see the same emotion in her eyes that I always see. It looks like pity and I don't want any. I had managed to forget about January for the last few refreshing, unchained hours. But now she's here and she's got that pity look in her eyes and it all comes flooding back. Let's tear the band aid off. I go up to her and greet her with a shy hello. An awkward moment passes as she fumbles with her words, unsure of what to say. I feel like a ghost, or some sort of monster, built by Frankenstein and back from the dead. The pity makes me feel that way, like what she's seeing in me must be terribly sad. She hugs me, too tight, I think trying to put the words she cannot say into the hug. I appreciate it, yes, but I miss regular hugs. Hugs without all the heavy, secret meaning. But then she pulls back, still holding onto my shoulders and she looks me straight in the eyes and she says, "I don't want to get into it or anything, but I'm glad you're alive," and it's perfect. It's just perfect. There are no questions I have to answer, we won't talk about it, and it's not a vapid nicety, just the truth. Even the pity in her eyes is gone. I

laugh and hug her back to me, perhaps a little too tightly.
"Me too," I say, "Me too."

In the hotel, I had been texting with Peter from Kenyan
Special Forces. When I was 'extracted' as they call it, I
think something got lost in translation because he was still
texting that he would come get me soon. I responded
telling him I was all set, that I had already left the hotel
premises and was very much alive. He seemed surprised
to hear that, and at first I wasn't sure why. Then he clarified that, after over twenty hours of the attack, two of the
terrorists were still alive. There was a concern, too, that
they also had suicide vests on, so it was difficult to 'eliminate' them. I cringed. The idea that that hell was still going on, that lives were still hanging in the balance, nearly
caused me to throw up. I had no idea how Peter was even
still standing after all the effort he had put in over the last
twenty plus hours, much less how he was still fighting
these men. I wasn't sure what to respond, so I thanked
him from the bottom of my heart for his hard work and
dedication and asked him to keep me updated.

4 weeks ATA: I need a shrink. A really, really good one.

A few hours later, Peter texted me that it was finally
over. That all the terrorists were dead. Dead, dead, dead.
I could have jumped for joy then. It was finally, by all def-
initions, totally and completely over. I texted him back
saying that he is a true hero, and that I would never forget
him or what he had done to save us. And I won't. I will
never forget Peter, or Carter, or Sam, or the man that's as
big as a house who doesn't know what to do when women

cry, or the KSF, or the British SAS guy I read about after the fact. I will never forget how many brave, heroic people came together that day to save my life, save all of our lives. I think of them every time I wake up, safe and sound in my own bed. I think of them when Paul hugs me, or I laugh with pure, unadulterated joy. I think of them every single day. I owe them so much more than I can ever put into words.

JOY CANNOT BE FELT IN THE WAKE OF GUILT, ANGER AND FEAR. That's why therapy is important. It has taken me dozens of hours of therapy and PE to shovel enough shit off myself to feel joy again, not just in special moments, but broadly, in the overpowering way I used to feel it, where my whole life looks magical instead of just a single instance. I read in Shantaram that "The worst things that people do to us always make us feel ashamed. The worst things that people do always strike at the part of us that wants to love the world. And a tiny part of the shame we feel, when we're violated, is the shame at being human." I want you to chew on that for a second because those words are extremely powerful. In the wake of horrible trauma, I think a common reaction is shame. I certainly felt it, and I often still do. But it took me a long time to take it one step further. To ask myself if I should really be carrying that shame, or if it should reside with my aggressors. To ask myself if I was simply carrying it because the terrorists refused to do so. To realize that as a victim, I didn't deserve to feel shame. What happened to me was not my fault. I have to unburden myself, because that shame is always trying to overtake me, trying to blind and cripple me, so I have to push back. I have to force my way through the quicksand of that shame, and the guilt and the

161

anger and the fear, because on the other side is the antithe-sis of all of those things: pure, true joy at being alive.

The woman who was escorting me around, after I had flights and had responded to texts and talked to Paul, asked if I was interested in a nap. I didn't want to sleep, I was still far too edgy, but I knew I should try. She told me there was a very safe housing complex right across the street where she could take us to nap, but I vehemently rejected the idea of leaving the Embassy, which was living up to its reputation as a safe bunker. She seemed sur-prised by my unwillingness, but she rolled with the punches and found some cots for us to rest on and set them up for us in a quiet corner of the building in two separate offices. As she was walking us over to them, I stopped at a little hallway table I was passing and looked down at the stack of newspapers. I froze in place. The pic-ture on the front was of a huge inferno, a massive flame completely encircled by smoke rising from a group of burning cars. I shuddered, and then I looked at her and asked if that was at the hotel. She jumped, startled, and started apologizing. She turned the newspapers over, say-ing I shouldn't have to look at that, and then chastising herself and the staff quietly, but aloud, noting that they had turned off all of the TVs but hadn't thought to grab the newspapers. I hadn't realized until that moment, but sure enough, there were many blank, black TV screens around. I had stopped listening. All I could see was the picture, the picture of the decimation I had heard, but not seen directly. The same decimation that had left chunks of human flesh outside my window. And the headline. The headline that said fourteen innocent people had lost their lives. Fourteen people, and I so easily could have been one of them. But somehow, I was standing there, alive, reflecting on the newspaper's account of what had happened to us. Reflecting on their lives, which had been lost so senselessly. Reflecting on what someone had texted me at some point: that one of those dead was a young, American CEO. A 9/11 survivor, who had lived through that tragic day only to die in a Kenyan hotel at the hands of terrorists eighteen years later. And wondering, as I would continue to, why the hell we do this to each other.

8 weeks ATA: I was on a plane today, and I watched Green Book. I find planes distinctly comforting, because it was on the plane that I was finally, genuinely, getting out of Africa alive. See how everything in my life is defined by the attack now? So I like to settle in and watch movies or read and enjoy these short hours where I feel ok. Where everyone around me has gone through genuine security screening. Where it's relatively unlikely that I will die at the hands of a suicide bomber. So I was watching Green Book, and there is a scene where the black protagonist goes to get a drink at a bar in the South and ends up having his life threatened by two white strangers. He's kind and educated and they're racist idiots and they want to kill him just because of the color of his skin, something he cannot control. And I thought, my god what would that feel like to have strangers want to kill you just because of something you cannot control? Uneducated, angry strangers, when you are unarmed, and you have not started a conflict at all. And then I realized: I know exactly what that feels like. Terrorism is not new. What was lynching?

I didn't sleep. I lay on that cot, looking out the window. It was a beautiful day, and that little corner office looked out onto this tall, grassy field. There were local people moving in and out of the grasses, harvesting something, I think. It was stunning, like out of a painting. But all I could do was wonder if the glass was bulletproof or not. Finally, the escorts came back to get us, and got us into our secure transport to the airport. We traveled with an armed guard, which helped ease my anxiety a little, but not much since the thought of waiting alone at the airport terrified me to my core. On the way, though, once again I found myself distracted by Tim's kind antics. He told me that his plan had been to go lion collaring after this (I still don't know what that means and am afraid to find out). But that there had been so many signs that he had finally relented and decided to head back to Georgia. See, when he was leaving Georgia in the first place, his plane had an issue with its landing gear, and it was so dire that the flight attendants gave the speech about bracing for impact and emergency landings. Then at the last minute, the pilot was able to get the landing gear down and they diverted and landed at another airport. Then, on the way to Kenya, a recent gardening injury on Tim's foot had started to swell and become infected. The antibiotics he had seemed to have no effect. When he finally got to Nairobi, he had called a doctor to his hotel to give him an injection to fight the infection, which was why he had been laid up in his room when the terrorists attacked. So he joked that he had finally gotten the message, apparently a far worse fate was waiting for him if he went lion collaring, it was time to head home. I laughed as he related this story, and as he concluded we pulled up to his terminal at the Nairobi Airport. All I could think was that I was so incredibly happy that his two kids would see him again, swollen foot and all. We didn't know how to say goodbye to one another, it was odd to be so closely bonded to someone by an insane and life-threatening experience, and yet only have actually known him for half a day. We hesitated, and then hugged and he told me it was great to meet me. I laughed and said that we might as well be honest, it was terrible meeting under these circumstances. We wished each other the best, and then I watched him walk into his terminal. He never looked back, and I was glad he didn't. He had told me that he comes to Nairobi regularly. As I sat there, watching him walk away, I hoped against all hope that he would never return.

1 week ATA: I never want Carolyn to come. I schedule these visits with her, where she comes over and talks to me about what I saw and what I am feeling, and she really is amazing, she always knows just what to say. And afterward I feel totally drained, emotionally exhausted, but it's a good thing because it leaves no room for fear or anger. So when we wrap one up, we always select the next time she should come. But then, as that one approaches, I start to panic. Talking about what I saw, what I felt, what I am feeling now, is too painful; it makes the whole thing feel too real, too close. I always cry to Paul, telling him I need to cancel, I can't see her, I can't do this. He always holds me tightly but tells me that he thinks maybe I am just nervous, and that the sessions always seem to help so he doesn't think I should cancel. It's almost funny, because I know he is right, but I can't change the dread in the pit of my stomach. I can't change how badly I want to cancel. I can't change how much I want to curl up on the couch and never fucking talk about any of this horrible shit again. But my instincts are wrong, and I know that. Talking about it will help me get better. Lying on the couch in tears will leave me stuck in this misery, in this depression, forever. Pushing it away and trying to live in denial will only make me worse. I have to fight my instincts and see her again. I have to talk more about what happened, not less. I have to recognize that what I think will be uncomfortable is actually growth. It's healing. Even though it hurts.

This driver handed me over to a woman who worked for the airport. She walked me over to the security line, but I started to have a panic attack when I realized the security line, which was so long that the estimated wait time was an hour, was outdoors. Outdoors. So anyone could walk up, say with a suicide vest on, and blow themselves up, and there would be absolutely nothing between us and them. In fact, someone in that line could already have a suicide vest on, and just be waiting for the right moment to detonate. I couldn't do it. I started hyperventilating, and I was trying desperately to explain to her that I couldn't wait in that line. Yet again, I didn't realize this was my new normal, I just thought my reaction was limited to the particular place, the fact that I was still in the country where my life had been threatened for so long, and that I still hadn't slept. When she realized what I was saying and processed that I had been in the hotel that had been attacked, this woman snapped into solution mode. She signaled to one of the airport agents and had a long conversation in a language I didn't understand. He kept shaking his head, but she kept nodding and gesturing at me, and finally he nodded, and she waved me over. They let me cut to the very front of the line, so it was a mere moment and quick bag scan before I was inside. Then the woman walked me to passport control. I was thanking her profusely for getting me through the security line so quickly, when I looked back and saw the guard putting an exit stamp in my passport. An exit stamp. It was true, then, I was leaving. I was leaving the country fully and completely alive. I broke down into sobs, and the woman escorting me had to help hold me up as my knees buckled. That exit stamp in my passport would always serve as a reminder that I can get through anything.

16 weeks ATA: I was reading more of that amazing book today, titled Shantaram. And I read a quote that roughly boils down to this: "As a Muslim, I have more in common with rational men and women of any other religion, even rational atheists, than with fanatics of my own religion." I rewound and listened to that quote repeatedly. It rang so incredibly true. Fanatics have perverted religion for as long as it has been around to use it to further their own goals to gain power or money. But if we make sweeping generalizations, if we try to say all followers of a religion that has had fanatics are fanatics themselves, then that would be every religious person on earth. It's not the way to think, and it's not the way to try to live peacefully. We have to see the fanatics for what they are. I will not generalize. I will not hold all the innocent Muslims accountable for what those Islamic extremists did in the hotel that day. Because the innocent Muslims are not responsible. And if I tried to persecute them for that act of terrorism, I would just be adding to the divi-

siveness in the world, adding to the foundation of what al-lows for acts like this to happen in the first place: hate. And I have no room in my life or in my heart for hate.

I flew business class back. I figured, if ever there was a time I needed a lie-flat seat to get some rest, it had to be after being awake for almost two full, consecutive days. My business class ticket meant that I had access to this amazing business class lounge, so that's where my airport escort dropped me off. It felt like I had never seen any-thing so clean, had never eaten food so delicious, had never experienced Wi-Fi so fast. It was bizarre to have all of those modern comforts back. I was still insanely jumpy, and my senses were straining all the time waiting for the next bomb to go off, but the tiredness reached a point of no return. It took over my consciousness, blurred my vi-sion and forced my eyelids shut. Finally, I caved and pushed two loungers together, curled up in a ball across them, and set an alarm for a few minutes before my boarding time. Then, for an amazing forty-five minutes, I slept. A dreamless, black, comforting, restful sleep.

7 days ATA: Today I was struck with an idea. When I had been heading out on this business trip, I had reached out to Google's security team via email, asking if they had any ad-vice or suggestions. They sent me a 'briefing doc' for Nairo-bi, which said things like, "Crime rates in Nairobi are high... However, the biggest risk to Googlers remains to be petty crime and road traffic accidents." It also listed recommend-ed hotels for Googlers to stay in, "security-assessed hotel(s)" it called them, which is how I had chosen the DusitD2 in the first place. I knew it was not a personal doc just for me, be-

cause I had seen other employees accessing it at the same time; this was something they kept on the shelf and sent out when asked about Nairobi specifically. I wanted to see what it said now, after my terrorist attack. My shock turned instantly to rage. It said in big bold letters at the top, "Update following 15/16 January hotel attack Nairobi: Based on our latest assessment, normal travel to Kenya, including Nairobi can continue." I closed my laptop hard, flung it across my room. I didn't want it anywhere near me. Didn't want them anywhere near me. They were sending people back! Telling employees it was safe to go there, just like they had told me. They had a new list of 'security-assessed' hotels, and they were operating business as usual, like nothing had happened. I hadn't died, and because I hadn't died, because brave strangers had risked their lives to save mine, Google had not had to change anything. My fucked-up head was nothing to them. I was nothing to them. The other employees heading to Nairobi, the ones that could die in the next attack, were nothing to them. The lives of the brave American men who would have to save the next employee were nothing to them. I am physically ill.

When I woke up, I had basic function back. Enough, in fact, to sit up and look at the TV, which of course was relating what had happened in the hotel. That was when I saw the new death toll. It had risen, from fourteen dead in the hotel, to twenty-one. The hostages. It had to be the hostages. Clearly more murder victims had been found now that the attack was finally all the way over, and they hadn't been part of the initial death toll, so that was the only thing I could figure. My stomach turned, and I felt like I was going to throw up. I didn't know what to do, and

I had no one to talk to. The only thing I could think to do was distract myself so I didn't fall apart. I had just a few minutes before I needed to go board my plane, so I opened Netflix to see if the Wi-Fi was good enough to stream. I watched a few minutes of a favorite show from childhood, and it was just enough to take my exhausted brain away from the thoughts of dead hostages. It was the first time I used my new coping mechanism: avoidance. Eventually I would learn that avoidance only makes things worse, even though it's the brain's natural response to trauma. But that day, I don't think I had any other options.

2 weeks ATA: Why do we need so badly to hate?

The trip back was a bit of a blur. It took me almost a full day to get halfway around the world, but most of what I remember is sleeping, eating and watching Friends on the planes. I did not think about the hotel. I thought only about my family, and how I was getting closer to seeing them, touching them, with every single moment that passed. I remember nearly laughing when I boarded my plane out of Nairobi and the business class flight attendant offered me champagne. I almost accepted, because it certainly felt like a moment worthy of celebration, but it was all I could do to get my seatbelt on before I passed out. I remember crying on my layover in Frankfurt when I saw how clean and organized the airport was, and the Polizei carrying their massive guns and enforcing absolute order. I remember after FaceTiming my parents in the business class lounge in Frankfurt that I stood up out of the little cubicle I had been in and pulled out my noise-canceling earbuds only to realize I had an audience. Every single other passenger in the lounge (only about a dozen since it was 5am local time) had turned around in their seats, mouths agape, as they had listened to me relate some of the details to my parents. I hadn't realized how shocking that must have been, or how much my voice was carrying.

I apologized for the noise, but no one responded until one woman just said, "You were in that hotel?!" When I nodded, she added, "Well, are you ok?!" I had no idea how to talk about the experience yet, especially with strangers, so I just nodded again and sort of ran away to board my next flight. Then in Chicago, my plane had landed early so my mom texted that if I ran to the gate, I could probably get on an earlier flight back to Ohio, because there was one that was boarding right at that instant. That would save me a two-hour layover in O'Hare, so I did as she said. The United agent was very nice and accommodating and moved me to that earlier flight. I hadn't told him what I had been through or why I wanted to get on the earlier flight, and he didn't ask, but when he gave me my new boarding pass I started sobbing profusely, and I will never forget the look of utter shock on his face. It almost made me laugh. I also later learned that by boarding that earlier flight, I had (accidentally) evaded the FBI, who would be waiting for me at the airport in Ohio at the time I had originally been slated to land, only to find that a girl fitting my description would not get off of that plane. It was a story that Carolyn and I would laugh heartily about the next week.

Sometimes now I can't remember pieces of the attack,

which is so strange. It was the most impactful day of my life, and yet the specifics or chronology of many events is a total mystery to me. So I don't know if everything in here is correct, historically, but I have done my best, using texts and news and other people's memories, to reconstruct it. At the end of the day, I can only tell you the story the way I remember it. Please just know that I did my best.

Walking through the airport in Ohio, everything feels like a dream. Am I really here? Did I really make it back? Am I really about to see, touch, hold the people I love most in the world? It doesn't feel like it can be real. Maybe this is heaven. I don't see anything around me. People are floating by me on either side, but I don't see them, I am just walking as fast as I can toward the exit. I know they will be there, my family, waiting. Over heads and through the thick of the crowd, I see a sign held high that says, "Welcome home!" It's written in sparkle letters, so I know my mom must be the creator, and she must be holding it up. It's bobbing up and down, she must be jumping. Paul is incredibly tall, so I see him first. His face is calm, victorious and pleased as he looks over the crowd trying to pick me out. I feel hot, happy tears start stinging my eyes as he searches for my face. I pick up my pace even more, I cannot wait to hug him. He spots me and his smile lights up his face. I can feel the warmth from it, and it is so incredibly touching. As a few people in front of me find their loved ones and step out of the way, I can finally see my mom and dad. When she sees me, my mom starts shrieking. There are no intelligible words, just these shrieks of joy and disbelief. It's incredibly loud and people around her go quiet, staring. She rushes toward me, blocking Paul's path and she grabs me, but as soon as her hands touch my shoulders, her knees buckle. My tears dry instantly as I hold her up, whispering soothing words into her ear. "It's ok momma, I'm here. I made it. It's ok, it's ok, we are together now, I'm here." I make eye contact with Paul who is standing behind my mom, and he smiles. I reach a hand out toward him, the other still holding my mom up, and he grabs it. My dad joins our misfit hug, and we all hold one another. We bask in being back together. We bask in the fact that I lived. My mom tells me that all she wanted was her baby back, and now she has that. She has everything she could ever want. I feel more joy and more hope in that moment than ever before in my life. And I know, from the bottom of my heart, that together, we will all be ok.

You know, living through a trauma does not make you appreciative every day. You don't just magically develop a new perspective and a newfound appreciation for every moment you spend alive on this earth. You don't wake up in the weeks after a trauma and look at your loved ones fondly and realize that you never stopped to smell the roses enough before and you really should. Nothing about healing is automatic. And nothing about developing a new perspective is easy. Even really wanting it is not enough. It takes work. Gnarly, grind-you-down, wear-you-out work. In the weeks after a trauma, you feel like it now defines you. Like it broke you. Like your new life will be made up of what little is left of you, because the trauma took everything else. It destroyed you. You think that at best, you might be able to live some sham of the life you had before. You might be able to fake it well enough for it to almost feel real. But one of the most horrible and liberating things about trauma, is that your life afterward is defined by you, and you alone. The trauma will want to control you, but it can't without your explicit permission. You are in control, even when you're broken and alone and crying on the living room floor. And with work, and therapy, and an incredible support system, you can process that trauma and put it the fuck in its place. So that your new life belongs to you and you alone. So that the trauma is part of you, but it does not define or control you. You control the role it plays in your life. And getting it processed and put away is more work than I can even put into words for you. But it sure as hell is worth it.

I used to think it's what you do in your most terrified moments that defines you. Now I know it's what you choose to do afterward.

Epilogue

40 Weeks ATA: How do you wrap up a story that you are still very much living? How do you put a neat bow on it, how do you look back and say quaint and eloquent platitudes about something that is still ongoing? The terrorist attack is a part of me, and it probably will be forever. It still very much affects the way I think, the way I act, the way I am. I still avoid hotels at all costs, and when I cannot avoid sleeping in one, my nightmares come back in full force, not only while I am staying there but for weeks afterward. I still can't watch the news, because every story is my story, every victim is me and the people who were with me in the hotel that day. I still jump, noticeably, when there is a loud unexpected noise, or when a dish is dropped at a restaurant. I still can't look my colleagues in the eyes without wanting to cry, because all I can think is that they might not be safe on their next business trip, and that my pain and suffering has done nothing to protect them. I still sob in my sessions with Dahlia each week. I still go through intense bouts of insomnia, which bring back my depression in spades, as well as many of the other parts of PTSD, like an inability to make any decision, no matter how small, or an obsession with the idea that life would be easier for everyone if I wasn't here. I will not paint you a picture that is rosier than my reality, because I think to do so would be a disservice to everyone who has ever experienced, or is currently experiencing, PTSD.

But that is not to say that there aren't some beautiful parts.

I wouldn't say that I have a new set of priorities, but I notice myself doing a better job staying true to them, not just in a broad sense, but in an everyday sense. I put the people in my life before everything else, whether it's my job, my work outs, my hobbies, anything. I have always prioritized loved ones, but it used to require more conscious effort. Now it happens automatically, without thought, because it is just so clear that they are the only thing that really matters. I know what it feels like to have everything else stripped away, to be willing to give everything else up just to see them again, and I know what it feels like to get them back after that. So there is no hesitation when I have the opportunity to put them first in my life. They are my everything.

I put less emphasis on climbing ladders in my career. I saw the emptiness in it when I was in my worst bouts of PTSD, and it feels like I saw the truth in it in that way. And more than anything else, I try, in any way I can, to bring hope and empathy, a sense of connection, to people experiencing PTSD. That journey might be the most deeply troubling yet touchingly beautiful one of all, because I have connected with people I never would have imagined

I would have anything in common with. I have realized that PTSD is rampant, and often undiagnosed. So many people think it can only affect veterans, and while it occurs at unbearably high rates in the military population, it also occurs in civilians. I am living proof of that, but I have also talked to cancer survivors, people given terminal diagnoses, sexual assault victims and so many more who have suffered or are suffering from nearly the same set of symptoms that made me want to stop living. When we talk about it, we soften, finishing each other's sentences, crying each other's tears, and reveling in the fact that we are not alone. We also take solace in the fact that if we lived through our trauma, and the subsequent PTSD, we can live through anything. And we bond over how much the experience still affects us, every day, and that no matter how much 'better' we get, sometimes the memory comes back in full force, bringing us instantly to our knees.

I had one of those moments just last month, and in many ways I am still reeling, battling the sleeplessness, the nervous ache in my stomach even as I write this.

The FBI flew Paul and me to New York to give us an update on my case. They wanted to fill us in on who had been arrested and what they had found out in the intervening months. I was terrified, knowing I would feel like I was right back in that hotel bathroom, but I was also hungry, almost desperate, for information. I wanted to hear them confirm, out loud, that every single terrorist who had set foot in the hotel that day was dead. Had died right there on that property. I had heard rumors afterward that some had lived, and they used to sneak out of those rumors and directly into my nightmares. I thought hearing the FBI say they were fully and completely dead, never to rise, might help me sleep again.

We flew to New York City on September 11, of all days. Terrorism and its devastating impact felt like they were all around me, inside of me, choking me so that I could not take a deep breath. I kept shifting on the plane, trying to get to a position where I could expand my lungs, take a breath that didn't send a sharp pain down into my ribs, but I had no luck. The ghosts I was carrying sat too heavily against my chest. The panic worsened as we cruised across the city in a taxi at sunset, heading toward our hotel. Hotel. I had to stay in a hotel, which was bad enough, but it was in New York City on September 11. It felt totally and completely fucked. As we entered the lobby, I fought down the panic, swallowing hard, willing myself to remember it was just a hotel, most hotels are safe, this is the US, response time would be fast if anything happened, I probably wouldn't die there.

Paul and I dropped off our bags and then stayed out until late, eating great food and trying to ignore my looming sense of dread, my increasing irritability. It was nearly poetic, the two of us, very much alive, walking around New York City on 9/11, holding hands and trying to keep the conversation topics light. I should have felt grateful probably, grateful to be alive and there and holding the hand of the man I love, the man I had finally actually married. I should have felt lucky to have made it through a terrorist attack myself and reflected on how fleeting life is, and thanked the stars that I still had mine. I should have stopped in the street, holding Paul's hand, and asked him to take a moment of silence for Jason Spindler, the American who died in the attack, who had himself been a 9/11 survivor.

I wish I had. But terror is tough to cut through. It is, as I now know so well, all-consuming. It eats up thoughts of everything else, it eats up who you are, or who you otherwise would be, and leaves only basic instincts. And if anything was sitting with me as we walked those streets, it was that: terror. I kept worrying that we were naïve for being there, that an attack was simply inevitable. I kept reflecting on the irony of the fact that we would likely die in a terrorist attack while in New York City trying to get information on the terrorist attack I had already lived through. I was battling with those thoughts so much that I barely spoke. I couldn't do much more than focus on how to keep myself looking calm, how to not cause a scene. I walked through the streets of New York City holding tight to Paul's hand and thinking only of the phrase that Paul often says to me as a joke when I remark that we are in a dicey situation: "At least we have each other." And in that way, I felt comfort and terror and joy and closeness and alienation all at once.

We went through the motions that next morning, getting ready, picking at breakfast, both without speaking to each other much, both without noticing. When we finally arrived at the building where we would meet with the FBI, after accidentally trying to break in the wrong door and causing some random strangers to nearly panic, we managed to find the lobby. There were six men standing there in suits, a pretty intimidating monochrome wall. By that point, Paul and I were running a few minutes late, which felt like hours given how on edge we were, so I tried to push past them apologetically, explaining I was late for a debrief. All of their expressions changed at once, from stern to soft, each smiling shyly as if they should be apologizing. They did not get out of my way, but explained in kind, too-quiet voices that they knew who I was, and that I was there to meet with them. They told us they could take us over to the conference room as soon as we turned in our devices, gesturing to the front desk.

I was distracted as I handed the man who sat there my phones and my laptop. I couldn't shake the feeling that I had seen one of those men before, and I was quite certain it had been in a movie, though I couldn't recall the title. I squinted, trying to see the movie again, see him in it. It also struck me as bizarre, one of these FBI agents used to star in movies?! That was quite the career change. I turned back around slowly, went up to him. I had to stop myself from asking which movies he had been in before, feeling like the question was too odd in that setting, so instead I just said, "I'm sorry, but you look extremely familiar." He was bashful. He looked at the floor for a moment before returning my gaze.

"Yeah," he said. "We've met before."

It clicked, and the weight of it nearly knocked me to the ground. We *had* met before. This guy had been the driver in the FBI vehicle that picked Tim and me up from the med eval on the side of the road in Nairobi. I hadn't recognized him without his FBI bulletproof vest. Or maybe it was just that I couldn't fully recognize him outside of Kenya, because he did not belong in my real ATA life. He didn't fit. He was a ghost from a very scary movie that I had seen thirty-some weeks before. That I had *lived* thirty-some weeks before. I thought for a moment that I might faint. But another instinct won out. I grabbed him in a huge hug. "I'm so happy you're here," I told him, crying softly onto his jacket. "I'm so happy you were there."

They led us down the hall, past pictures of astonishing men saving people from extraordinary situations. Past medals and awards and plaques, to a very average looking conference room. There were water bottles set out at each place, and I snatched one up as I sat down, desperate for something to do with my hands. I can't tell you much of what they told us in that room, but I can tell you that they were kind and incredibly helpful. I can tell you that they have been working diligently every day since January 16 to hunt down the people who orchestrated this attack, and to keep Nairobi safe, keep Americans safe. I can tell you that I felt more at ease in that room than I had in months, even while we reviewed every sharp and painful detail of those seventeen hours and the days and weeks and months afterward. I can tell you that after answering all my questions, they asked if there was anything else on my mind, and all I could say was, "Thank you." It is because of people like them that most terrorist attacks are thwarted. It is because of people like them that I can stay in a hotel in New York City on September 11, and walk out unharmed, physically and mentally, the next day. It is because of people like them, and their counterparts in other organizations, both in and outside of the military, that I am so goddamn proud to be an American.

Do you see what I mean now about the epilogue? About the neat bow? I can't conceal the fact that the attack is inherently intertwined with my past, present and future with a few final wise words. I can only say that all I can do each day, all any of us can do, is put one foot in front of the other. So that's what I will continue to do.

1 year ATA: I am sitting on a bed in a hotel room waiting for him to show up. Paul is getting him, and his girlfriend I think, from the lobby. I am shaking all over, not because I am in a hotel (I can stay in hotels fine these days), and not even from the irony of meeting him in a hotel room, but from sheer overwhelming torrents of emotion. This is the man who saved me. This is the man without whom I would literally be dead. This is the man who kept the Dusit from being a repeat of Westgate. He kept the attack to seventeen hours instead of several days. He made it so that the building wasn't leveled with explosives and he allowed hundreds of us to get out alive. This is Obi Wan Nairobi, and I am about to meet him in real life.

The actual story had only been related to me recently, and there was one thought that consumed my consciousness at that moment: they weren't sweaty. The Americans who had come to my door, they weren't sweaty. They hadn't looked worn out, they didn't have streaks of god-knows-what on their clothing or skin. They looked almost freshly show-ered. Which was what made the truth of the real story crash down on me all at once: the Americans hadn't been involved with the terrorists. They had been in the lobby, true, and had communicated updates to me and others for hours, up-dates that genuinely had probably been the saving grace that kept me from going fully insane, for which I will always be deeply grateful, but that had been the extent of their in-volvement. It dawned on me for the first time somehow that there had to have been other men, up there on the top floor, who had been dodging explosions and bullets. There had to have been other men who had ultimately taken the lives of the terrorists and saved our lives, saved my life. But then as I listened to the details that were being reiterated to me, I realized something even more astounding: there had been one man. One off-duty SAS operator who had been the first responder to the scene, and then for a long time, the only responder. It was him showing up that had driven the terrorists to cease their systematic executions and retreat to their fallback positions. This one man had literally pressed pause on the murders of innocent civilians with his willingness to intervene. One extraordinarily brave man, who happened to, as he would say later, "have been training for this my whole life." One man who led every single action that was taken against the terrorists. One man who was responsible for their demise. One man who hadn't even donned ear protection or eye protection in his haste to save us, and who had assumed that he would be advising the responders who were sure to be on site, but when he found no one there, hadn't even hesitated before beginning to clear the buildings. It was bizarre, but only as bizarre as the day itself had been, and more importantly, it was true. His name is Christian Craighead, and like his Star Wars-themed nickname implies, he had been our only hope.

I hear the door open, but I hesitate before turning around. How do you thank a total stranger for saving you? How do you meet the man who risked his life for over twenty hours to save yours? How do you put into words what his bravery means to you? How do you meet Superman in a hotel room in DC? As I swivel on my feet, I almost recognize him. Not from that day, we never saw each other then, but from all the photos we have looked at since of him in his balaclava pulling people out of the hotel. I can picture him as he was in those photos, purple button-down shirt and trendy jeans on, piercing blue eyes completely focused on the task at hand, gear showing the Blackbeard's Flag logo that adorns my now-favorite thermos. But this man standing awkwardly in the door of my hotel room has no gear. No bulletproof vest, no rifle. His hands are in his pockets and his shoulders are slightly shrugged, evidence of the fact that neither one of us has any idea what the hell to say in this kind of situation. What even is this 'kind' of situation? I am drawn to him by a single urge: hug this man. Put your head on his shoulder as you have dreamt of doing so many times and sob, thank him for what he did in whatever words you can think of. I grab him by the shoulders and pull him tight to me, hugging him as if for dear life. I can think of no words at all in this moment, ironic because I am a blabbermouth, so we just stand in an embrace for several moments and that says it all. When he pulls away - I would have held on forever, I think, so it's good that he thinks to end it - he goes past me toward the couch and I hug his girlfriend, too. She says they are so happy to be here, and I laugh a little; I am the one who is happy to have them here! I walk with her over to the couch and chairs where Chris is already sitting and just barely catch him wiping his eyes. He is here, in my hotel room, this hero, and I have no idea what to do. I hand him the letter I wrote him the night before which tells him about my family, my brother, my parents, the wedding I got to have, and all the other things he gave back to me a year ago when he saved my life. He starts the conversation, thankfully, by mentioning some of his memories from that day. We start a process of comparing notes, almost, asking each other about what was heard and seen at different times. Inter-

186

estingly, this seems like catharsis for both of us. He shows me pictures he took on his phone of the dead terrorists and somehow this is the most comforting thing I have seen in a year. We reread texts and compare timelines. He explains that the rhythmic thudding I heard was a sledgehammer attempting to pierce the roof of the top floor of the hotel, which is where the terrorists were, so that they could be exterminated from above. I hadn't realized, but part of my mind had always been wondering about this, and it's finally able to rest. He asks me and Paul how we have coped, and we tell him the truth, that it's been hard at times but that we are so incredibly thankful that we have lives to live together! We ask him the same and are surprised to find that he is haunted by that day. He says he has relived it every single day since. He looks down at his hands as he says this, and I want to hug him again, but I resist. I am alarmed that he would struggle with the memories of that day when he should exult in them, should take pride in all the lives he saved. He says he replays it over and over, wondering what he should have done differently. This is not only terrible, it's relatable because of course I do the same. We are somehow two halves of the same whole, irrevocably shaped by that fateful day, though we never crossed paths officially. He was on the outside, I was on the inside, and together we are a picture of the full story, a story that forever marked us, scarred us, connected us. I try to tell him that it's crazy for him to beat himself up over it, to think instead of me, and the hundreds more like me, all of whom he saved, living our lives only because he stood between us and evil. He tells us about his life and how every moment of it seemed to lead him to the hotel that day. He tells us how he will be retiring soon, his military career now feeling fully complete.

We spend the weekend in DC, just being near him every second that he will put up with us. I get nervous around him and tend to stammer, and my idolatry clearly makes him uncomfortable, humble man that he is, but I can't help it. All I can see when I look at him is what would have happened without him. I know that he is the literal difference between the vision I saw at first: the terrorists busting my door down and murdering me, and the vision that ultimately came true: the Americans getting me off the property safely. He is the dividing line between good and evil. He is, to put it lightly, my hero. I've never wanted kids before, but I start contemplating having a son so that I can name him after this hero, to pay some sort of homage to this lifesaver. He doesn't seem to want any of this, though. He doesn't want to be famous or recognized - in fact, he has spent time in the aftermath of the attack making sure he isn't identified, as his whole career has always depended on his ability to stay anonymous and out of the limelight. He just wants to talk to us, to discuss that day with people who understand it, and perhaps to be reminded that he did the right thing. Reminded that he doesn't need to contemplate what he could have done differently, because what he did allowed this girl to be sitting in front of him, with her now-husband, crying tears of joy at odd intervals and making him uncomfortable worshipping him like this.

We talk about the ripple effect. We talk about how he joined the military the same year I was born, and he worked his way up to special forces. He ended up being a specialist in close quarters combat, particularly in times when hostages need to be saved. Every element of his training and experience came in handy that day, helped him save us. We talk about how opportunity met preparedness, and how he didn't hesitate before going into the attack alone. We talk about how the fact that he saved me made me quit my job and create an app that helps people heal from PTSD, and that it made Paul take a new job that contributes to our government. That because of him we have changed everything about our lives and are trying to dedicate them to leaving a positive legacy in the world. In his honor. And we are only the representation of a tiny segment of the people he saved that day. We talk about how much good is being and will continue to be created by what he did. What he represented. What he showed us. We talk about life and love and meaning. And to anyone passing us, we are just a group of friends chatting in a bar. The girl, she seems a little too drunk, she keeps tearing up. The British guy has a thick accent, and it's funny because he gets harder to understand as he finishes each drink. The other guy is way too sober; he looks serious as hell. What a ragtag crew. No one knows what we have all been through, both together and apart. They don't know that the British guy irrevocably changed our lives, and in a way, we his. They don't know the meaning of these three people sitting at this sticky table in this dark bar, and how amazing it is that they are alive and together. But we know. And that is all that matters.

For Chris's full story, be sure to grab a copy of his book, *One Man In* and follow him on Instagram *@christian_craighead*

To share your story, send thoughts on the book, or ask me questions, connect with me on Instagram *@meylichapin*

If you think you have PTSD, I encourage you to find help. Try my iOS app Trauma Brace, a therapist, or both. *You can get better.*

Acknowledgments

Thank you to Christian Craighead, without whom there would be no book because there would be no me. Everything I am, and everything I achieve or am able to give back, is truly thanks to you. You are my hero, and my own personal superman.

Thank you to my wonderful husband Paul who really is my rock. Thank you for always believing in me and my dreams enough for the both of us.

Thank you to my parents, for your unconditional love and support.

Thank you to my brother for being the first one to explain to me what was happening in my mind after I got back from the attack, and for always keeping me sane.

Thank you, Adam Ross, for being my first reader! You gave me the confidence to actually try to get this thing published, so I really wouldn't be here without you.

Thank you to the Andersons for being our California family, for giving me a place to live while I wrote this book, and for surrounding us with hugs and laughter even in the toughest of times.

Thank you to Lauryann for spending Thursdays with me. In my darkest days, this was one of the only stable elements of my life that I could always look forward to. It gave me a reason to get out of bed, and without that I never would have been able to write this book.

To Diane Shader Smith, for your relentless commitment to publishing and publicizing *Salt in my Soul*, and the personal help and support you somehow provided to me amidst all of that, thank you. Without you, and without that book, I never would have believed that I could get here. You are a force of nature, and you inspire me every single day.

To Debbie, Christina and Monica, my gurus on this journey. I can never put into words how much you each helped me. I love you all, and each one of you, in your own way, saved me. Thank you.

To all the amazing people at the FBI who worked with me (I am not supposed to mention your names, but you know who you are), thank you for your unending support, the thousands of questions you answered for me, and for being the support system my employer was not.

To the men and women who serve in the military, at home and in our allied nations, your bravery is unparalleled, as is what you contribute to the world. I can only get out of bed each day and face the world because in the back of my mind I know that you exist, and that you are willing to make the ultimate sacrifice to preserve our freedom and justice. There are no words I can say to truly thank you for that, but know that I am awestruck at your impact on this world.